The Practice
of Kindness

The Practice of Kindness

Meditations for Bringing More Peace, Love, and Compassion into Daily Life

The Editors of Conari Press
Foreword by Rabbi Harold Kushner

Conari Press
Berkeley, CA

Printed in the United States of America on re-cycled paper

Conari Press books are distributed by Publishers Group West

ISBN: 1-57324-028-1

Cover illustration by Anthony D'Agostino
Cover design by Shelley Firth

Library of Congress Cataloging-in-Publication Data

The practice of kindness : meditations for bringing more
  peace, love, and compassion into daily life / the
  editors of Conari Press ; foreword by Harold Kushner.
       p.   cm.
    ISBN 1-57324-028-1
    1. Kindness.   2. Simplicity.   3. Love.   4. Caring.
  5. Spiritual life.   I. Conari Press.
  BJ1533.K5P73 1996
  177'.7—dc20   95-46125
                                                      CIP

$\mathcal{W}$e wish to gratefully acknowledge all those who helped in birthing this book:

Brenda Knight, whose inspired idea this was and who provided many seeds for meditations; Will Glennon, who wrote most of them, and Mary Jane Ryan, who wrote some and edited all of them; Shelley Firth, for cover design; Anthony D'Agostino, for angelic illustration; David Wells, for superior interior layout; Ame Beanland, for production proficiency; Emily Miles and Erin McCune, for publicity prowess; Elizabeth von Radics, copy editor supreme; Donna Scism for proficient proofreading; Banta Company for perfect printing; the rest of the Conari team who keep things going: Jennifer Brontsema, Everton Lopez, Molly Kattenberg, Tom King, Claudia Schaab, Ralston Soong, Eric Wells; our dedicated interns past and present; Nancy Briggin, Random Acts of Kindness Week coordinator; the folks at PGW, our distributor, who get our books out into the world; all the authors whose thoughts are quoted here, and particularly Conari kindness teachers
Daphne Rose Kingma,
Dawna Markova,
and Sue Patton Thoele.

"Even as a mother protects with her life / Her child, her only child, / So with a boundless heart / Should one cherish all living beings; / Radiating kindness over the entire world."

—*The Buddha*

ℑhe Practice of Kindness

"Humans are powerful spiritual beings meant to create good on the earth. This good isn't usually accomplished in bold actions, but in singular acts of kindness between people. It's the little things that count, because they are more spontaneous and show who you truly are."

—*Dannion Brinkley*

Foreword

Rabbi Harold Kushner

Oscar Wilde once wrote, "the nicest feeling in the world comes when you do a good deed anonymously, and somebody finds out." The great virtue of the classic bestselling *Random Acts of Kindness* series and of this successor volume with which I am honored to be associated is that they redeem so many acts of kindness from anonymity. We do something good and in many cases no one recognizes it or thanks us for it, and we are left to wonder "what's the point of going out of my way to be good if no one cares?" These books teach us that many people do, in fact, care. Their content, and their reception by a public thirsty for such stories, teach us two valuable lessons.

The first is that performing an act of kindness is a tonic for the one who performs it. It is a cornerstone of my faith that, just as our bodies are made so that certain foods and certain habits are healthy and others are unhealthy, so are our souls made so that certain kinds of behavior nourish the soul and other kinds are toxic. Human beings were fashioned to be friendly, honest, and helpful to each other. When we act that way, when we resist temptation, when we go out of our way to do a favor for someone, we feel right. Something inside us says, "Yes, this is the way a person is meant to feel." When we are deceitful or jealous, we are acting against our nature, and we have to work hard to resist the message our bodies and souls try to send us.

Some years ago, Duke University Medical Center did a study of Type-A personalities, the aggressive, hard-driving people who are always trying to get ahead and do several things at a time. They wanted to study whether such behavior affected a person's cardiovascular system. What they learned was this: if you are a Type-A because you enjoy the challenge of making things happen and knowing that they turned out well because of your efforts, you'll be fine. But if you believe that it's a jungle out there, that everyone is out to get you if you don't get them first, that constant hostility and suspicion will wear you down and diminish your life in both length and quality. Being kind to others is a way of being good to yourself.

The second great lesson of *Random Acts of Kindness* and *The Practice of Kindness* is that when you are kind to others, it not only changes you—it changes the world. Cumulative acts of kindness change the emotional climate in which we live. They teach people to see the world differently.

A woman has a flat tire while driving in a rainstorm. Two teenagers come along and offer to change her tire. That brief encounter will permanently change the way that woman thinks about life and about young people. She will tell her friends about it and change their outlook as well. She will share the story with her own children and increase the chances that they grow up to be teenagers who will stop to help a motorist in trouble.

A teacher in an inner-city public school notices a spark of lively intelligence in one of her pupils that poverty and hunger have not been able to extinguish. She encourages that child, buying her food and books out of her own pocket. That child grows up to be a doctor, a nurse, an athlete, a politician, and becomes a role model for thousands. How do we measure the impact of the good deeds we do?

Being in a totally dark room can be frightening, until we discover how little light we need to banish a roomful of darkness. The pain, the hopelessness of the world, may look insurmountable until we move to counter them with our little deeds of kindness.

Why did God create the world and fill it with such erratic, unpredictable creatures as we human beings are? One Jewish tradition would have it that God made the world the way it is so that we would have the possibility of being nice to each other. The Talmud teaches that "when a person does a good deed when he or she didn't have to, God looks down and smiles and says, 'For this moment alone, it was worth creating the world.'"

When we go out of our way to be kind to someone, in large ways or small, our reward is the knowledge that we have redeemed the world.

The Sphere of Kindness

Since the publication of *Random Acts of Kindness*, we have received more than ten thousand letters from people, telling us their kindness stories. In addition, during the hundreds of wonderful call-in radio shows we have done, we have been privileged to hear the stories and thoughts of thousands of eager callers from all across the country. Each person's story, each act of kindness was unique and powerfully inspirational. Yet even while it is clear that kindness is flourishing, many people wondered what they could do to help build a movement of kindness in their community; they also asked for specific suggestions for things they could do to bring more kindness into their lives.

As book publishers, we were at first somewhat unsure how to respond, but as the requests piled up it became clear to us that there was something we could do in each of these areas. The first, finding a way to facilitate what was an obvious groundswell of support for a kindness movement, was well outside our area of expertise, but we decided to dive in anyway. We declared the week of February 12 through 18, 1995, to be the first annual Random Acts of Kindness Week, hired a national coordinator, and set up a very loosely organized campaign to encourage and support local communities in their efforts to celebrate the power of kindness.

The results were overwhelming—literally and figuratively. Spearheaded by schools, churches, and an army of dedicated volunteers, Random Acts of Kindness Week was celebrated in virtually every state. In all, 140 towns and cities—from Los Angeles and New York to Yukon, Oklahoma, and Wilton, Connecticut—rallied to spread the philosophy of love and caring. Joined by millions of individuals throughout North America, participants perpetrated acts of kindness with wild abandon.

So overwhelming was the response that as Random Acts of Kindness Week approached,

Conari Press was effectively subsumed into Kindness Central. It put an enormous strain on our publishing business but was worth every exhausting moment. In order to keep Random Acts of Kindness Week going, and stay in the publishing business at the same time, we have created the Random Acts of Kindness Foundation as a separate, nonprofit entity to coordinate and expand participation in this annual celebration of kindness. (For more information on how you can partici-pate, see the back of this book.)

As for the second request—specific advice on things people could do to bring more kind-ness into their lives—we realized that our position as the central clearinghouse of so many wonderful stories had in fact provided us with the resources we needed to offer some suggestions. The result is *The Practice of Kindness*, a book of meditations to take kind-ness to a deeper level.

At first, we tried to sift through the stories and pull out a list of specific actions, but we ended up with what we thought was a relatively sterile and uninspiring list. It looked and felt too much like a compilation of rules; and by its very nature, kindness cannot be reduced to rules. Rather, it springs instead from a generosity of spirit and is acted out within the specific context of the moment. (Which is why you will find many paradoxes within these pages—one minute exhorting you to "just do it" and the next saying you've got to give up trying. Both are true.)

So instead, we began to think about the incredibly rich variety of ways that kindness manifests itself in the world and the effects such manifestations can have. We turned once again to the inspirational words of the many writers and spiritual leaders who have championed kindness in their lives and used their quotes to focus in on its wealth of nuances. Each quote is followed by a story that shows how that particular aspect of kindness is played out within the context of an individual's life and a meditation focal point for the day.

As the pages unfolded, we began to see

that the practice of kindness has two dimensions. One is vertical, in which we deepen our connection to ourselves; the other is horizontal, in which we reach out to connect to others. Together, they create a sphere, the symbol of wholeness. Both are limitless, for there is no end to how deep or how wide you can go. But you can't have one without the other, for to serve others is to bring your wholeness—including your woundedness and your shadow—to the wholeness in others and in life.

Each meditation gives both a concept and a context that can, upon reflection, lead you into deeper understanding of and preparation for both of these dimensions. It is our fervent hope that they assist us all to better see and respond to the opportunities we are given to bring more kindness into our lives— and into those of all with whom we inhabit this fragile home.

Kindness
is an Attitude
and an Action

"Since you get more joy out of giving joy to others, you should put a good deal of thought into the happiness that you are able to give."

—Eleanor Roosevelt

$\mathcal{A}$s we move through our lives, we carry with us the accumulated experiences that mold our attitudes and our behavior. When we are young and inexperienced, we are often more vulnerable to being pulled in different directions by the events of life. One bad experience, in which our trust is betrayed, our generosity scorned, or our love rejected, can cause us to build unconscious defenses that have the unintended effect of isolating us, of making us fearful or tentative; and that can cause us to pull back from the world.

Later, as we grow in maturity and wisdom, we learn that although we cannot choose what life will deliver to us, we *can* choose how we will respond. As we begin to live our lives more consciously—going back and sifting through the events that helped shape our lives, examining how and why different emotions are triggered in our hearts—we can begin to build an entirely new framework for who we want to be, instead of simply accepting who we ended up being.

Through this deeper understanding of the

events that have influenced our lives, of the values we hold most dear, and of the things we need to be happy, we can begin the exciting process of taking control of our lives. At the most fundamental level, this begins with the conscious choice of how we wish to be in the world. From that solid foundation, we can act freely and fearlessly, knowing that our actions will reflect our being out into the world.

The practices in this section focus on the intricate underpinnings of a strong foundation of kindness and will assist you in your exploration of how to release that kindness into the world through your actions.

Start Now

"I spent four years 'getting ready' to start a diet. I'd get brochures for weight-control programs and look them over while eating a pastrami sandwich. I'd buy the latest diet books and read them with a bowl of chips. My losing weight was such a topic of conversation that finally—over a substantial lunch at my favorite Italian restaurant—my best friend got so exasperated she said, "If you really want to lose weight, then put that damn fork down right now!" Shocked, I dropped the fork and just sat there with my mouth hanging open. When I closed my mouth, I realized I had started my diet."

Most of us carry around an image of ourselves as we would like to be—a little thinner or stronger, more patient and reliable. But what we want to be means nothing until we stop intending and start acting.

Like dieting, when it comes to the practice of kindness, right now is the best time to begin. It doesn't require much work or sacrifice—no giving up desserts, no one hundred leg lifts, no pushing a rock up a steep hill. Just a commitment, right here and now, to smile at the bank teller, give a kind word to the grocery checker, let the driver in front of you cut in. Simple, really.

Remember What's Important

> "In the end, nothing we do or say in this lifetime will matter as much as the way we have loved one another."
> —*Daphne Rose Kingma*

In the hustle and bustle of our busy days, full of faxes, phone calls, and a thousand and one errands, it's really easy to get caught up in the daily details and forget what's important in life. Often it takes some kind of trauma—the death of a loved one, divorce, a life-threatening illness—to wake us up to what matters. After all, no one on his or her death bed regretted not spending more time at the office.

Fortunately, we don't have to be facing a personal tragedy to make our relationships our number one priority. No project, no deadline, no clean kitchen is as important as the quality of your relationship with the person sitting across from you at the breakfast table, as the child who needs your attention right this second, as the mother who is alone in the nursing home.

Remembering what's important gives us the graciousness to take the time, make the phone call, send the card, not say the bitter retort on the tip of our tongue. When we re-member what's important, we generate more loving-kindness in our lives.

Take the Risk

"In the long run, we get no more than we have been willing to risk giving."
—*Sheldon Kopp*

"When I was in second grade, a new boy, Derrick, showed up halfway through the year. He had a bad leg, and all the kids teased him. I never teased him, but I was afraid of being too nice to him because I didn't want the other kids to think I was a sissy or whatever second-graders think.

"That summer my mom made me take swimming lessons at the city pool and Derrick was always there. He was a great swimmer, and I found out later that he swam every day to build up strength in his legs. One day during a break in lessons, I was sitting on the side of the pool and he swam up and said hi and thanked me for not teasing him at school. I said something like, 'oh, no big deal,' but inside I felt like a jerk for being afraid to be friendly with him. Now I'm in fourth grade and Derrick is my best friend. In fact, he's the best friend anyone could ever want."

So many of us are so afraid of one another—of having our hearts crushed (again), our spirits broken—that we miss out on the love and connection that is available if we would only take the risk. Acts of love and kindness *are* risky—we risk looking foolish or being rejected; we risk being laughed at or ignored. But if we *don't* act, we risk losing even more—the potential for love, for friendship, for communion with another soul. Today, take a risk with just one person.

Accent the Positive

"People deal too much with the negative, with what is wrong. . . . Why not try and see positive things, to just touch those things and make them bloom?
—*Thich Nhat Hanh*

"I had one of those days when everything went wrong. It started when I was late for work, wound its way through a mountain of irritated customers, computer breakdowns, short-tempered colleagues, car trouble on the interstate which found me walking to a telephone in a drenching thunderstorm without my umbrella, and ended in a totally irrational and emotionally bruising fight with my husband.

"I ran out of the house, trying somehow to outrun all my problems, but the dark cloud just hung over me. As I walked through our neighborhood remembering all the bad things that had happened that day, the storm that had so rudely soaked me earlier began to clear. I came around a corner that overlooked a valley and was treated to one of the most beautiful sights I have ever seen: The clouds had thinned to long, tailing wisps and were floating gracefully apart like some kind of celestial doorway, and the biggest full moon I had ever seen was slowly moving into view. I watched as the light from the moon passed like a hand over the valley, turning the entire rain-soaked valley into a kaleidoscope of reflected light. I just started laughing and crying at the same time. Here I was mired in my own little dirt clod and was being so magnificently reminded by the night sky that there was much more to life than what I was feeling in the moment."

We are very clever at finding everything that is wrong. And once discovered, we get stuck, like a deer caught in the headlights, intensely focusing on it. In order to be kind to ourselves, we need to learn to see our problems in their real context—to open our eyes and hearts wide enough to drink in all the beauty and joy that is always around us, no matter what is going on.

Don't Let Fear Stand in Your Way

"Do not be afraid."—*Jesus*

Several decades ago, sociologist Pitarim Sorokin, who founded the Institute for Creative Altruism at Harvard, identified five obstacles to love: fear, stress, limitations, self-devaluation, and tribal altruism. Not surprisingly, they are also the obstacles to kindness.

When we are afraid, we contract—our muscles tighten, our vision narrows, we physically pull away. In other words, we retreat into a private world, cut off from human connection. When we are stressed, we operate like an robot on the fritz—twitching physically and emotionally, obsessively focused on the narrow issues that are causing our stress, unable to see, much less reach out to, others. When we believe that we are limited, ineffectual, we seal ourselves in a cocoon of apathy. When we see ourselves as "not good enough," we constantly re-create a lonely and self-limiting world.

The last obstacle to love and kindness is the most complex: tribal altruism—the sense that the small group is more important than the whole. Tribal altruism is the driving force behind racial conflict, religious intolerance, and war. It is also the dangerous halfway house we can become stuck in when practicing kindness.

When we first overcome our fear, stress, sense of limitation, and self-devaluation to extend kindness to others, we often start with what is near to us—our family, our "tribe," our religious group, our local community, our nation. But if we stop there, we risk the danger of perpetuating greater harm to the whole of humanity in the name of love for our smaller group. It is only when we can move beyond all five obstacles, when we can see every man, woman, and child as a precious and indispensable part of humanity, that we bring the practice of kindness to its fruition.

What obstacles to kindness do you most often experience? Today, just notice what blocks the free flow of kindness in your own life.

Just Act

> "Where we've gotten mixed up is that we believe actions follow belief. But experience creates belief."
>
> —*Reverend Cecil Williams*

"I've always thought of myself as a good person who wanted to do something to make a positive difference in the world. But for years I was paralyzed by the sheer scope of the world's problems; they seemed so overwhelming to me. In the midst of my private despair, I happened to have lunch with a friend who mentioned that he had been volunteering at a local food project, and he asked if I would be interested in helping out occasionally. His request surprised me. I realized that I wanted to help, but at the same time it just seemed to be so futile. I asked him how he managed to keep his spirits up when the lines of hungry people kept growing.

"He smiled and said, 'I have to confess, part of the reason I do this is because it *is* what keeps my spirits up. I can't solve the problem of hunger in the world, but when I am working in that kitchen, knowing that every plate of food I prepare is going to feed someone who really needs it, I feel more alive, more like the man I want to be."

It is so easy to get lost in the circular motion of our own thoughts that we forget that it is our *actions* that set everything—including our thoughts—in motion. Even the most insignificant-seeming action reverberates out into the world, setting off a continuously self-perpetuating chain reaction.

We don't have to believe that what we are doing will have a significant impact or even make a tiny difference. All we need to do is *act*—to begin and watch what happens.

Give Up Keeping Score

> "Blessed are those who can give without remembering."
>
> —Elizabeth Bibesco

"Coming home from work the other day, I saw a woman trying to turn onto the main street and having very little luck because the traffic was a constant stream. I slowed and allowed her to turn in front of me. I was feeling pretty good until, a couple of blocks later, she stopped to let a few more cars into the line, causing us both to miss the next light. I found myself completely irritated at her. How dare she slow me down after I had so graciously let her into traffic! Even as I was sitting there stewing, I realized how ridiculous I was being. Suddenly, something Jon Kabat-Zinn wrote in *Wherever You Go, There You Are* came floating into my mind: 'I heard someone define *ethics* as "obedience to the unenforceable. . . ." You do it for inner reasons, not because someone is keeping score or because you will be punished if you don't.' I realized that I had wanted a tit for tat: If I do this nice thing for you, you (or someone) will do an equally nice thing for me."

Kindness is the currency of our hearts, the only currency that can never be subtracted and never be balanced in anyone's ledgers. We choose to be kind because it is the way we want to live our lives, not because we will be rewarded in some way. When we start to keep score, we become closed-hearted: I'm not doing anything nice until someone does something good for me.

Our acts of kindness are whole unto themselves. They require no acknowledgment and no reward, for the act itself returns us once again to the heart of our own humanity.

Make of Yourself a Vessel

> "Pain can be an incubator for compassion if we keep our intention toward healing, learning, and serving."
>
> —*Sue Patton Thoele*

"There is an old woman in our town who is simply incredible. She has lived a very difficult life, full of suffering. Two of her children died, one from a terrible lingering disease and the other in an automobile accident. Her husband had a very bad stroke many years ago and then lingered on for twenty years before dying. Yet she is the most generous and compassionate person I have ever met.

"One day, I asked her how she could still wake up every day with a smile and a kind word for everyone around her. She looked at me with this really surprised expression on her face and said, 'Oh, but my life has been full of so many wonderful people. We all have our troubles, but those are only doorways we must walk through. Each of the terrible things that happened to me also brough͟[t] unexpected surprises—moments of conn[ec]tion with others, opportunities to become a better person. I guess I do wish it could have been easier, but really I feel that my life has been blessed nonetheless.'"

When times are tough, it's easy to shut out the rest of the world. And sometimes it is necessary to turn inward, feeling the depth and breadth of our sorrow so that our wounds can heal.

But, ultimately, we need to come back out into the light, scars and all, and allow our suffering to make us more compassionate toward others. Precisely *because* we have known pain, we can empathize more truthfully with the pain of those around us; we can offer the example of our own journey to healing as encouragement for those still taking the first steps. In so doing, we not only inspire fellow sufferers, we make sense of our own pain.

Rather than close off our hearts and sink into despair, we can let hardship hone us into a vessel overflowing with wisdom and compassion. And there's no doubt that the world could use more of that!

"... rd a guess as to the most en-
... prevalent anxiety among human
...ngs—including fear of death, aban-
...donment, loneliness—nothing is more
prevalent than the fear of one another."
—R. D. Laing

When we are very young, we fearlessly devour our world and reach out to people with eagerness. As we grow up, surrounded by the daily outpouring of bad news, we become more and more afraid and too often end up retreating farther and farther into our isolated shells. We find ourselves looking at the world in terms of control, possessions, and power instead of growth, understanding, and feeling. But we can begin to connect again.

"Every time I went to the grocery store," wrote a woman named Molly, "I passed this homeless woman who seemed to be living on a bench in front of the store. She never said anything, but she was dirty and I felt threatened somehow. At first I would hurry past her, but it started to bother me. I was angry at her for being there, but I was also upset with myself for getting so flustered.

"Gradually I began to give her whatever loose change I had. One day, I stopped and talked to her just long enough to introduce myself and learn her name. After that we would always smile and great each other by name. It may sound strange, but I began to look forward to seeing her smile and ask me how I was doing.

"One day, I sat with her for a while, and she told me a little about her life and how she had gotten to this place. She told me it was people like me—those people who were still willing to see her as a person—who gave her the strength to keep trying. All the way home I thought of her and realized that she had shaken me out of my tiny little world and, in a way I can't easily describe, had made my life much richer."

Like Molly, to break out of our shells and return to the joyful richness of life, we need to become fearless again. We *can* reach out and share in one another's experience—who knows what amazing thing will happen as a consequence. Try talking today to a stranger and see what magic is created.

Let Go of Outcome

> "It reeks of paradox. The only way you can do anything of value is to have the effort come out of non-doing and to let go of caring whether it will be of use or not."
> —Jon Kabat-Zinn

"One day last year, my daughter took a handful of roses to school with the intent of simply handing them out to random students. After she had given out a few, she was mobbed by students all begging for a rose. She gave them all away but told me later that night that at first it had felt bad because 'That's not the way I had planned it,' she said. By the time we talked, however, she had already recovered, and at the end of our conversation, she laughed and said, 'Dad, you should have seen all those girls' eyes begging for a rose.'"

We act with compassion and kindness because we want to be the kind of people who do, not because we have an expectation that it will have a certain effect. When we are invested in outcomes, we will inevitably be disappointed: The person won't necessarily be healed by our kind gesture; the world won't be "fixed" by our grand effort. So long as we are focused on outcomes, we will not receive the deepest benefit of our actions—that resonant feeling that reminds us that, if only for that moment, we are all one.

Don't Give Up

> "It is only necessary to know that love is a direction and not a state of the soul. If one is unaware of this, one falls into despair at the first onslaught of affliction."
> —Simone Weil

"Last year, I read *Random Acts of Kindness*, and it had a very powerful effect on me. It felt like I was being reminded of something very important that I had forgotten. At the time I read it, my younger brother (who can be an unbelievable pest) had pushed me to the point where I was being really mean to him.

"After reading the book, I promised myself I would treat my brother well even when he was at his pestering worst. For a while it worked really well. He was surprised (and suspicious), and I felt so much better about both of us. Then one day when I was upset about something that had happened at school, he started in on me big time. I completely snapped and called him a 'slimy little creep.' It shocked both of us so much we just stood there with our mouths hanging open, staring at each other.

"I felt terrible, because I know it really hurt him and also because I had broken my promise to myself. Later, I apologized to him and that helped, but I still felt bad until I realized that sometimes I'm going to mess up. After all, I'm only sixteen."

We will fail. It is an unavoidable part of our human nature. No matter our commitment to being kind and loving, we will gossip behind someone's back, snap at our child, say something intentionally cruel to our spouse. But that's no excuse not to keep trying. If we beat ourselves up over our failings, we tend to get discouraged and give up. But when we remember that love is a direction and not a fixed destination, we simply pick up the compass of kindness and begin again.

Make Each Day Count

"I want to convince you that you must learn to make every act count, since you are going to be here for only a short while."
—Don Juan

Have you ever met someone who has had a near-death experience or a life-threatening illness? Usually, they are filled with more love, compassion, and joie de vivre than the ordinary person. There seems to be something about a close brush with death that creates an awareness of the preciousness of each day, of loved ones, and of life itself.

"My brother-in-law used to be the black hole of the family. He just sucked up everybody's energy, complained like mad, and never gave anything back. We were always rescuing him from various scrapes and receiving precious little thanks. Then, when he was thirty-seven, he was hospitalized with a very rare brain tumor. For a couple of months, it was touch-and-go as to whether he would survive at all and, if so, how much brain damage would be done. Fortunately, he made it out just fine, and the amazing thing is that when he got out of the hospital, he was a completely changed man. Now he's the one who brightens up every family occasion with his humor and positiveness, the one all the kids gravitate to. He has become more responsible toward his family and is consistently grateful for anything you might do for him. The difference is like night and day."

We don't have to almost die to learn to make every day count. We can each learn to live as if this is the only day we will have—for it might be; we never know. We can offer the loving words, the giant hug, the soulful glance we would give if this were our last day on earth. For even if we are still here tomorrow (and chances are pretty good we will be), only good will have been done by offering our love today.

Abandon Guilt

> "You can feel for people and . . . still want to have a nice sweater."
>
> —Joan Rivers

So many times we don't want to do anything about the suffering in the world because deep in our hearts we fear we will have to give up our comfortable lives, go off to Calcutta, and live like Mother Teresa. We don't want to—and we feel guilty about it.

The practice of kindness does not require extraordinary gestures. When you practice kindness, you simply try to bring happiness and joy to those you meet on your daily path. You don't have to sleep on the street or give away all your possessions; in fact, you don't have to give up anything—except guilt. Guilt is the paralyzing emotion. Guilt stops the flow of love. For generally, when we feel bad that we aren't helping, we can't do anything helpful at all.

Love and kindness are not physical things that will be lost or diminished when they are given. They are instead like the miraculously abundant and sustaining loaves and fishes that Jesus distributed to the multitudes who had come to hear him speak. Each act of kindness comes from the bottomless well of love and adds to the abundance of magnanimity in the world.

In such a expansive view, guilt is nowhere to be found. We simply do what we can, when we can, where we can, as lightly as we can.

It's Never Too Late

> "It doesn't matter how long we may have been stuck in a sense of our limitations. If we go into a darkened room and turn on the light, it doesn't matter if the room has been dark for a day, or a week, or ten thousand years—we turn on the light and it is illumined. Once we contact our capacity for love and happiness . . . the light has been turned on."
>
> —*Sharon Salzberg*

"At work a few weeks ago, I sat in on a presentation from a local nonprofit that helps underprivileged kids. The man giving the talk was someone I had gone to high school with and, at that time, he was the most cynical guy I had ever met. Afterward, he came over to me with a big smile on his face and said, 'Bet you never imagined I'd end up here.'

"We went out and talked for a couple of hours. I found out that he had been heavy into drugs, jailed countless times, and finally ended up in a maximum-security prison for seven years. He told me that if I thought he was mean in high school, I should have seen him later. 'I was the original angry man, so mad at anything and everything, I didn't even know who I was anymore.' Then, in prison, he got drafted into an experimental group therapy project, and the man who ran it changed his life. 'He didn't do anything special, he just treated me like a human being, and suddenly I started wanting to *be* a human being.' At that point, he laughed: 'There I was, sitting in this prison cell and feeling like I had just crawled out from under a rock into the most beautiful spring morning imaginable.'"

We are all born with the capacity for great kindness—it is deeply woven into the very texture of our souls. But sometimes, before we can access it, it takes effort and the kindness of others to clear away all the debris we have accumulated through living. Is there a person in your life who, with a little kindness from you, can find that capacity in herself? Is it you who needs to believe more in your own innate goodness?

Give Up Trying

> "Try? There is no try. There is only do or do not do."
> —*Yoda, in* The Empire Strikes Back

So many of us say we're "trying"—trying to be more considerate of others, to take time for ourselves, to find the time to make a difference in the world—but "try" as we might, we never really get around to it. That's because *saying* we're trying is the great escape from *doing*. We want to excuse ourselves for not doing *and* we want to avoid looking at the real reasons that have kept us from following through: "It's not our fault that we haven't done it, 'cause we're trying." We don't go any further with it, and nothing really changes. When all we can manage is "trying," there is inevitably something else, something hidden or at least unexamined, that is really preventing us from doing what we want to do.

So next time you hear yourself saying, "I'm trying," take a moment to look at what is standing in your way of *doing* this thing you say you want to do. Is it that you are motivated by guilt—thinking that you "should" be doing it rather than being propelled by any sense that you want to? Do you perhaps feel pressured by others, rather than from your own inner desires? Are you afraid that doing it will make you too vulnerable, or that you will fail? Or is it that you really don't feel like being kind because you are too angry at the world—or someone in particular?

The old habits and personal issues that can keep us locked into a limited and lonely existence can be difficult to sort through and even more difficult to shed, but we can never find our way until we at least face them squarely. If you find yourself "trying," stop and search instead for puppeteer behind the curtain.

$\mathcal{Y}$ou'll Know What to Do

> "The words we need will come of themselves. When the words we want to use shoot up of themselves, we get a new song."
>
> —*Orpin Galiz*

"I've never been good with words. I'm always stumbling around, trying to find the words that will communicate what I really want to say, and half the time end up feeling like a complete idiot. Once when I was in college, I was out on a date with this guy I really liked, and I was so afraid that I'd blurt out something stupid that I hardly said a word all evening. The more worried I got, the more paralyzed I got. At the end of the date, he looked at me and said, 'Are you all right?' I was mortified. I knew I had blown it completely and before I could stop myself, I stammered, 'No, I'm not—I scared to death I'll make a fool of myself.'

"My date looked at me with this very mischievous smile and said, 'Well, you've done a pretty good job of it.' It was so funny and so exactly to the point, we both just burst out laughing. That, of course, broke the ice and enabled both of us to be more real with one another. It was great."

So often what keeps us from extending a kind word or deed is that we are afraid we won't say or do "the right thing." So we do nothing. But honest interactions, true meaningful connections between two people, whether old friends or total strangers, aren't an oral exam; they are the spontaneous exchange of our inner selves.

Kindness is not something you have to struggle to formulate. You need only let down what defenses might be in place and see what wells up from inside you.

ℋold the Possibility

> "If you can imagine it, / you can create it, / if you can dream it, / you can become it."
>
> —*William Arthur Ward*

"My second child died when he was four," recalled Clea. "It was such a devastating experience that it took me years to recover. My whole life seemed to have suddenly gone from bright Technicolor to drab shades of gray. Just getting up in the morning was a major undertaking. I couldn't understand how this could happen, and I had no hopes for the future. It seemed like everything was empty of meaning and feeling. After wallowing for six months in grief and depression, my younger sister came to me and told me it was time to start living again. She told me that I had to fix a picture in my mind of a day in the future when the sun was shining and I was playing with my daughter, laughing and having fun. She told me that even if it seemed impossible, I still had to imagine it could be true.

"I tried, but it was very difficult. After a

48

while I could see it, but it seemed buried in shadows. Gradually, the picture became more and more clear to me until, indeed, the day came when I did feel exactly as I had imagined. Then more and more days began to feel like that."

Fortunately, not all of us have to go through what Clea did. But we each hold the capacity to draw toward ourselves the things we want in life through envisioning their possibility— even if right now they seem impossible. If you desire more love, compassion, and peace of mind in your life, you can begin to create that reality by holding the possibility of being more loving, compassionate, and peaceful. What would a picture of what you want look like? Make it as detailed as possible and take a moment each day for the next week to imagine it.

Recognize the Value of Each Person

> "In a certain sense, every single human soul has more meaning and value than the whole of history."
>
> —Nicholas Berdyaev

It is a common theme of myths, legends, and biblical stories—*Cinderella*, *Beauty and the Beast*, the unwashed peasant boy who pulled the sword from the stone, the carpenter's son— that every individual carries in his or her soul the radiance of a princess, the enduring heart of a lover, the majesty of a king, and the seed of the Almighty. It is a common theme because we need to be reminded of it as often as possible. For, engrossed in our daily toil, we often lose track of this simple and astounding miracle—the beauty, dignity, and worth of each and every human being.

We are all inexperienced adventurers born into this world with nothing but our extraordinary potential and a wide community of fellow travelers. We then must each seek out the path that will make our lives joyful and fulfilling. But when we become too engrossed in ourselves, we can develop an overinflated sense of ourselves and lose track of the precious nature of our fellow adventurers. When we are able to remember, when we can see and accept each other as we really are, we naturally want to lend a hand; for who wouldn't want to assist the miraculous human beings we encounter on our journey?

There's an added bonus to remembering the value of others. When we see only ourselves, we walk alone, weighed down by our burdens. When we recognize we are all in this together, our steps are lighter and our hearts more joyful, for we have a world of resources to fall back on.

ℒearn a Little More Each Day

> "Kindness is wisdom. There is none in life but needs it and may learn."
> —*Phillip J. Bailey*

The practice of kindness is, above all, a learning process, one in which you learn more and more about yourself.

Rita is a good example. She was inspired by her minister to begin delivering meals to AIDS patients once a week in a welfare hotel. At first, walking down the long, dingy, foul-smelling corridors, she was afraid that she would be harmed in some way and would shove the food into people's hands as soon as they answered the door. As time went on, she began to feel more comfortable and would take a moment to smile or say hello. But then, suddenly, the fear would return. Sometimes, she was annoyed if a thank-you wasn't forthcoming. Often, she felt that she was "such a good person" to take on this task. Other times, she felt herself to be simply a tiny part of a vast organism that ceaselessly fed these people seven days a week, 365 days a year. As the weeks went on, she came to see so much about herself: fear, the desire for recognition, pride, compassion. A whole kaleidoscope of ever-changing reactions. "What was most surprising," she revealed, "was to see just how sanctimonious and righteous I was in doing this thing that took less than one hour of my time a week. My ego about it was enormous—and recognizing that did nothing to deflate it."

What comes up for you when you practice kindness? Do you want a reward? Recognition? Do you do it to feel good about yourself or because it is needed? Today, do something kind and notice its effect—on you, on the other person. What does that teach you about your capacity to give? Make no judgment about yourself. Just notice.

Do It Again and Again

"There are never enough 'I love you's."
—*Lenny Bruce*

"My relationship with my father has always been difficult. It's hard to have a relationship to a man who is never there. He is always in a such a hurry to go somewhere else. Almost all my childhood memories of him include watching him rush out the door. A few years ago, I got this incredible letter from him, telling me how much he loved me and how sorry he was for not being there for me. I still have the letter, and every time I read it I absolutely know that he meant every word. I called him the night I got it and told him how much I appreciated it, but we only got to talk for a few minutes because he was on his way somewhere. I called back a few days later and left a message on his answering machine. He didn't call back."

Just as intentions mean nothing until they are converted into action, so our actions cannot grow to their full potential unless they become a consistent part of our lives. So many men believe that if they send flowers once to their wives that covers for a year. So many women believe they should get eternal brownie points for once not complaining when their husbands watch football. But when it comes to doing good deeds, once is never enough.

Through consistent practice, one day at a time, we can turn kindness into a habit and ourselves into beacons of light for those who come into contact with us.

Kindness Begins at Home

"It is more blessed to give than to receive,
so give to yourself as much as you can,
as often as you can."

—La Verne Porter Wheatley Perry

$\mathcal{K}$indness truly begins at home, because the source of all kindness is the human heart, and an impoverished heart has little to give. It would seem simple enough, but in a culture where the words *self-centered* have come to carry a negative connotation, it is anything but. All too often, in our zeal to raise good, well-behaved children, we instill in them a strong sense of the importance of treating others well, but woefully neglect the essential first step—teaching them how to be comfortably centered within themselves. Also, because of our long cultural tradition of placing women in a subservient role to men, it is not surprising that women much more than men find themselves lost in service to others.

It is one of the most fundamental paradoxes of human existence that we live our lives as unique individuals, and yet the deepest spiritual meaning of our lives resides in our connection to all things. In our hunger for meaning, we spend our lives reaching out, striving to nurture those connections, and all too often we fail—not because our intentions were wrong, but because, like a tree with shallow roots, our foundations are too weak to sustain our reach.

In order to attain the peace of mind and happiness we seek, in order to joyfully assume our place in the process of creation, we must begin by tending and nourishing our own hearts. The unique identity we have been given is our vessel, our means of navigating the wondrous mysteries of creation and of delivering our gifts to the world. When we care for ourselves, when we are able to treat ourselves with kindness and respect, we gather the strength and confidence to love and love fully and powerfully.

The practices in this section help us cultivate kindness toward ourselves so that we can then extend our reach first to those close by us and then farther and farther out into the world.

Start Where You Are

> "What is required is a willingness to look deeply at one's present moments, no matter what they hold, in a spirit of generosity, kindness toward oneself, and openness toward what might be possible."
>
> —Jon Kabat-Zinn

"I was in a dead-end relationship, smoking two packs a day, eating too much, and walking around in a cloud of depression. I hated myself. I hated my body; I hated my rotten attitude; I hated what I had become; and every time I tried to do anything positive—diet, exercise, cheer up, quit smoking—I'd last for a few days and then fall apart and hate myself even more.

"One day when I was working up the determination to quit smoking again, my sister—who was always on my case to quit—bought me a pack of cigarettes and told me if I was ready to give up something, then I should give up being so hard on myself. At first I thought she was being sarcastic. When I realized she was dead serious, I started to cry. It turned out to be a lot harder than I ever imagined, but it was a beginning—the real beginning of my life."

All change begins with awareness. If you wish to cultivate more simplicity, love, and peace of mind in your life through the practice of kindness, the place to begin is an examination of where you are. The key is to look kindly upon yourself—to hold in nonjudgmental awareness just where you are right now in your life. For example: Oh, I do blow up if things don't go my way. Isn't that interesting. I wonder what that is about? I wonder if I can find a more positive way to express that . . .

The paradox is that when we begin to notice, without judgment, just where we are, we create the space for something different to happen. By treating ourselves with the kindness of acceptance, we make it possible to be transformed.

Love Yourself That You Might Love Your Neighbor

> "Service is a process of self-realization. . . .
> It's not love your neighbor as yourself;
> rather, you love your neighbor as you love
> yourself."
> —*Edgar Mitchell, former Apollo astronaut*

"Self-esteem has always been a big problem for me," explains Gina. "I never did anything right: I couldn't get the grades my brother got; I wasn't popular like my younger sister. It seems like all the years I spent growing up were one long chain of complaints and disappointments. I compensated by trying desperately to make people like me. I'd do anything for a kind word. At work I was the one who always brought in the home-baked cookies or arranged the birthday parties. Not because I wanted to bring happiness or joy, but as a desperate plea to be liked.

"At our staff Christmas party one year, this guy I worked with got really drunk and, after I had made some joke, looked at me and said,

'You are such a phony.' Later he apologized, but he was right. It was like being slapped in the face and suddenly coming to your senses. I had been living in some kind of pathetic dream world, where if I tried hard enough to be nice to everyone I would finally get what I needed. That was the moment I decided that I had to stop looking for approval from those around me and seek it in myself."

As Gina found out the hard way, the more you accept yourself, the more you are able to genuinely love others. Accepting yourself is not always easy, but it is a necessary first step toward caring for others: This is who I am, where I am, where I stumble; these are the ways I fall short, the hard edges I would like to smooth.

Knowing ourselves *and* being willing to accept the whole package—including foibles, flaws, and failings—is the first step in living an authentic and aware life. And from that deep well of compassion we find for ourselves when we truly face who we are can spring a genuine awareness of all those with whom we share the extraordinary experience of being alive.

Don't Forget Yourself

> "You can search throughout the entire universe for someone who is more deserving of your love and affection than you are yourself, and that person is not to be found anywhere. You yourself, as much as anybody in the entire universe, deserve your love and affection."
>
> —*The Buddha*

"I went back to Vietnam last year. I'm not really sure why I went—it just seemed terribly important that I go. When I think about it now, I think I went back to try to find something that I had lost there twenty-three years ago. It was a very strange trip, very disorienting. So much had changed and so much was exactly as it had been. I was there for five days, and most of the time I just wandered around in a fog to places I had spent time, places I had fought. On the last day, I was taking a cab to the airport, and the taxi driver started talking to me. He obviously knew I was an American and he asked me if I had fought in Vietnam. When I said yes, I was almost overcome with grief and shame. As I handed him his money at the airport, he held onto my hand for a moment and said, 'I was your enemy but now I am your friend.'

"On the flight back, I felt more alive than I had in years. If that cab driver in Ho Chi Minh City could hold my hand as a friend, then maybe I could be my friend as well."

Because we are human, we will all stumble and fall, be selfish and petty, speak sharply, and do what feels like the inexcusable thing. And because we are human, we all need and deserve compassion in order to grow and blossom. Of course it is wonderful when we receive such life-enhancing gifts from someone else, but we need to remember also to offer these qualities to ourselves. We deserve our own love just as much as anyone else does.

When it comes to cultivating love, kindness, and compassion, don't forget yourself!

Give Yourself What You Offer Others

"Treat yourself at least as well as you treat other people."

—*Theodore Rubin*

"Being nice was a big thing in my family, especially for the girls. We were taught early and reminded often that we had to be nice—even if it meant letting our brat of a brother play with our favorite toy. I think that Mom meant well, but it took me the longest time before I realized that all my 'nice' training was turning me into an angry and bitter martyr. It was so ingrained that I deferred to anyone and everyone about just about everything. Ask me where I wanted to go for dinner, and I would immediately say, 'Oh, I don't care, where do *you* want to go?' The question, 'Would you mind?' was always immediately followed by an 'Of course not!' Then later I'd find myself being resentful at being 'forced' into the situation.

"After years of this, I finally got it that I was as worthy of as much consideration as I granted the other person. Instead of merely deferring, I began to ask myself what did I really want and to offer the truth of that to the other person, even if it wasn't 'nice.' Slowly I stopped being resentful."

Kindness is a bottomless fountain—not a river running outward. True kindness cannot be given away, it can only be shared; and in order to share the grace of kindness, we need to partake of it as well. One of the most difficult tasks facing many people today is being able to treat ourselves kindly, to direct inward all the compassion and understanding we so often muster for a friend, sister, child, or spouse.

If this is true for you, how about getting in the habit of asking yourself what you want out of this day, what you need to make your heart sing, and then try to give to yourself in the true spirit of kindness.

$\mathcal{A}$sk What's Right

> "We need to dwarf our troubles and magnify our blessings."
>
> —Humphrey B. Neill

"I have a friend who has had a life from hell. She's the oldest of five kids and her parents are both alcoholics who gave up on life very early. Both parents are in and out of bars, institutions, jails, and occasional stretches of living out of cars, and they call her on a weekly basis, begging for money. Her younger brothers and sisters grew up without anyone but her to provide any love and guidance, much less clothes or food, and, as one can imagine, that has taken a tremendous toll on them. Meanwhile, she works as a secretary, making a bare subsistence salary, and goes to college at night. She is always exhausted, always being dragged by some family member into the middle of whatever crisis of the moment is going on.

"She is also one of the sweetest, strongest, and most generous people I have ever met. Sometimes when I hear the latest story, I ask her how she manages to keep going, and she always tells me, 'Sometimes it is really hard, but then I look around and realize that at least I know who I am and am trying to get what I need. There are so many people out there who have it so much worse, so many people who don't even have a clear idea of how to get on with their lives.'"

Life can be full of pain and hardship, but it is also a garden of extraordinary beauty and joy. It is so temptingly easy to just focus on what is wrong, no matter how large, without appreciating and being thankful for what is right, no matter how small. But when we do that, life seems to shrink down to the level of our discontent, and we make ourselves miserable on top of whatever true difficulty is occurring.

That's why a true act of kindness to ourselves is to celebrate and accentuate the positive in our lives. When we are able to live from a place of thankfulness, possibilities seem to open, and the world itself seems inviting and tantalizing. So right now, no matter what is going on in your life, ask yourself what's right and count your blessings.

Offer Kind Words

> "One kind word can warm three winter months."
>
> —*Japanese proverb*

Have you ever noticed what happens when you say something nice to someone—"That's a beautiful shirt," "You did a great job," "Thank you for coming into my life"—it's like pouring water on a wilted plant? No matter what is going on, immediately the recipient perks up: Her face glows, a smile appears, and she looks like the weight of the world is off her shoulders, if only for a moment.

"The other day I was walking back to work from lunch with my head down, brooding over my own misery, and I ran smack into a tiny old man coming out of a store and knocked him down. I was so embarrassed I could hardly speak. He picked himself up, smiled at me, and said, 'Thank you, young lady, that's more excitement than I've had in months.' It was so unexpected, I burst out laughing, and he smiled again. As he was walking away, he turned back to me and said,

'You have a very beautiful laugh, use it often.' It was the most wonderful thing anyone has ever said to me."

Kind words in the form of appreciation, praise, and admiration are the cheapest gifts you can give. And chances are, the more you offer compliments and praise, the more it comes back to you as well.

So don't be stingy with thoughtful words. A steady stream of genuine gratitude and appreciation goes a long way toward keeping our lives moist with delight, warm with the glow of love.

Refrain from Harmful Speech

> "The Sufis advise us to speak only after our words have managed to pass through three gates. At the first gate, we ask ourselves, 'Are these words true?' If so, we let them pass on; if not, back they go. At the second gate, we ask, 'Are they necessary?' At the last gate, we ask, 'Are they kind?'"
>
> —*Eknath Easwaran*

"I have a really bad habit—my mouth flies open before my mind gets engaged. I've always been like this; I guess I've always thought of it as part of my charm—I can be a very entertaining conversationalist. But lately I've begun to notice that I have also left a lot of wounded people in my wake.

"I guess what finally woke me up was when my witty retort send my younger brother running from the room in tears. He's fifteen years younger than me and has always looked up to me. In retrospect, I'm ashamed to admit that all this time I just accepted his adoration as my due and never even considered the responsibility I owed him. My 'clever' comment devastated him and there just is no excuse for that. I apologized to him later that day, but I think now I need to go back and thank him, because his reaction finally convinced me that I need to close my mouth at least long enough for my mind to catch up."

Kindness is found not just in actions and in words, but also in inaction and silence. We may not often think about that because it's hard to notice. After all, if someone bites his tongue and doesn't make a cutting remark, we will never know we could have been hurt but were spared by his kindness. But the Sufi rule of speech is a good one—if we all used kindness as a speech "barrier," much less negativity would be verbalized.

Of course, because people are all wonderfully imperfect beings, we will make mistakes and say things that we don't mean out of hurt and frustration. If we are the receiver of such misguided barbs, we don't have to react to them with equal venom. It is so much kinder if we simply choose to let them disappear without reaction.

Don't Forget Those Closest to You

> "I would like to have engraved inside every wedding band BE KIND TO ONE ANOTHER. This is the Golden Rule of marriage and the secret of making love last through the years."
>
> —Randolph Ray

There was a funny car ad on television a few years ago in which a couple—obviously in the middle of a fight—start opening and slamming the car doors as they yell at each other. In the background, a beautiful voice is very softly singing, "You always hurt the ones you love." It was funny, but it was also a little too true to laugh at.

How is it that we can go through our lives being kind and considerate to all those people around us whom we barely know, but snap at, curse, ridicule, and mistreat those we love the most? Paradoxically, it seems the very power of deep intimate love can sometimes make it much *more* difficult to be kind to our beloved.

One reason is because of our vulnerability in love. When we love someone, he *can* hurt us so much more than others because with him our deepest wounds are exposed. That very fact all too often puts us on the defensive and makes us overly sensitive to any and every perceived affront. In the grip of this defense, we forget that the very existence of that precious love is an invitation to an ever-deepening understanding and connection, and that kindness is the medium and the instrument of that transformation.

It's easy to be kind when nothing is at risk. By consciously exercising your ability to react with greater compassion and understanding with your spouse and children, you will fill your heart to overflowing and all the world will benefit.

Remember Your Parents

> "We have enjoined man to show kindness
> to his parents."
>
> —*Koran*, 46:15

"Like a lot of people, I've had some difficult times with my parents, especially my dad. He was like a piece of granite—harder than anything and completely unmovable without a bulldozer. Growing up meant doing things his way or paying the price. I guess part of the price was a teenage rebellion I am still thankful I survived. I left home on my eighteenth birthday and cut myself off from my parents as completely as I could. I think it was really necessary for me to figure out who I was, but it hurt my mom a lot and she kept after me. Eventually, she and I worked things out, but my dad wasn't going to budge, and I sure didn't feel like bending over backward to accommodate him.

"We went on like that for years. Then, when I was thirty-five, my dad died of a heart attack. I was completely unprepared for how strongly it affected me. I hadn't talked to him for seventeen years, but when I got the letter from Mom, I cried uncontrollably for hours. I guess inside I always thought there would be time. Now he's gone and later never came. The worst part is that I know I am as much to blame as he was."

It's so easy to be angry at our parents for all the ways they have failed us. And while it is important to understand and properly tend and protect the wounds we received, it is equally important to be able to accept our parents for who they are—faults and all. We need to love them for all the good things they provided us with and for all the difficult times they have had to work through. And perhaps someday even to appreciate that some of their failings that affected us most dramatically are the very things that made us strong.

Let the Children Lead Us

"And the children say blessings upon you."
—*Rainer Maria Rilke*

It's an old story, one that has no doubt been replayed millions of times over, but one that deserves to retold at every opportunity. The details change, but the heart of it remains the same.

In this version, it's about an old man in a corner house. He was a widower of some years and as ornery and contentious as could be imagined. For reasons no one but he knew, he was angry at the world and everything in it. Everyone in the neighborhood made a wide detour around his yard—everyone except the five-year-old girl who lived next door. At first, it was almost funny to watch. She would greet him with a cheery smile every time she saw him, and get back a gruff "harrumpf." She'd ask him to come play with her, and he'd turn away, muttering to himself. She'd retrieve his newspaper from the bush the paper boy always aimed for, and he'd be peeking out the corner of his window.

Over time, an almost miraculous transformation took over. The man began to look forward to her trek across the yard. He started coming out to take the newspaper from her hand. Eventually, he started to respond to her hello. Right now, they are together on the sidewalk. The old man is teaching her how to ride a two-wheeler, and they are both laughing.

Children are the wisest of all when it comes to kindness. The kindness of children is an astonishment, like poetry from a pure heart. Perhaps the very best thing we can do to cultivate kindness is to follow the examples of the little ones in our midst.

Become a
Miracle Worker

"I need a miracle every day!"
—*Jerry Garcia*

"My daughter's best friend is going to college, and it took only a small miracle. She graduated third in her class and was immediately accepted by the state university, but even with living at home with her single mother and figuring in student loans, there was no way she could afford the cost of tuition and books. She was resigned to getting a job and going to night school, but someone in town heard about her plight and had other ideas. After a very discreet flurry of phone calls, a trust fund was collected through hundreds of small donations. The package containing the trust fund papers, all made out in her name and to be paid out over four years, arrived yesterday. She came by to show us and couldn't stop crying and laughing."

What would it mean if you were to perform a miracle in someone's life today? It could be something as simple as taking the day off from work and taking your daughter to the park. Or spending time with one of your elderly aunts who has been left alone. Or hiring one of the needy neighbor kids to do some work in your garden. Or writing a thank-you letter to a teacher who helped you when you really needed it. So many little kindnesses we can offer are truly miracles in the other person's eyes. Consider yourself a miracle worker today and see what you can generate.

Begin with Your Feelings

> "The source of all energy, passion, motivation, and an internally generated desire to do good work is our own feelings about what we are doing."
>
> —Peter Block

"I made a discovery late in life that astounds me to this day. It is very simple, basic, and powerful. I married late and had my first child at age thirty-five. That baby girl reconnected me to the very core of my feelings with such power and such ease, it was like being plugged into a socket after a lifetime of running on batteries. I'd find myself giggling and laughing at nothing more than her tiny hand curled around my finger. And the feeling would last all day long. Everyone I knew was amazed at the changes that came over me.

"At first, it was disorienting because suddenly all these feelings were sprouting up all over the place and I didn't always know how to react. It even scared me sometimes because, being such a novice at this, I wasn't always sure I could handle all that emotion. But gradually I learned that everything I felt was like a very simple and very pure message to myself. It may sound obvious, but for men especially it is a profound learning—the more attention I paid to how I was feeling, the more I liked myself and the more I found myself acting like the man I wanted to be."

Our feelings are our direct link to our hearts. Everything of importance and lasting value begins there. The better we get at allowing those feelings to surface, at understanding and honoring the messages they carry, the more alive we will be, the more we will feel joy, happiness, and peace of mind in each and every moment.

Rather than battering ourselves with "shoulds"—I should be nicer to my brother; I should volunteer to chaperon the school dance—why not try following your true feelings about what you *want* to do. Connect to what gives you a sense of excitement, happiness, and gratitude for being alive; and you will spread positive feelings wherever you go.

Respect Your Limits

> "Feeling resentful and used in our relationships plays havoc with our ability to be warm and loving."
> —Sue Patton Thoele

"In my high-school yearbook, everyone wrote a sentence about what they wanted to be in life. My answer was that I wanted to be a good person. I guess I picked exactly the guy to test my resolve when I got married. I tried very hard to live up to my own expectations. Even though we both worked, I did the lion's share of the housework because he 'needed his relaxation.' I cheerfully put up with weekends and evenings alone because he 'needed time with the guys' or it was 'important' for his work. I deferred to whatever he wanted; I put my own needs and my own dreams aside so much that I forgot what they were.

"Over time, I found that despite all my efforts to be kind I was becoming increasingly angry and resentful. I guess I'm a slow learner. It took ten years of my building anger and his calling me 'selfish' before the charade fell apart. I had gone way beyond my own limits and felt as dried up as an old sponge."

Kindness comes from an overflow of the heart. It cannot be performed as duty, extracted by guilt, or induced by fear because what is taken by duty, guilt, and fear empties the heart and leaves us impoverished.

To live with a full and overflowing heart so that we can be kind to others, we must tend to our own needs and nourish our own dreams. This means understanding our boundaries and gently and lovingly setting limits. It is not selfish to do so—it is the essential caring for oneself that makes it possible for us to care for others.

Honor Your Need to Retreat

> "The people who have made the most contributions to the world have followed cycles of withdrawal and return."
> —*Arnold Toynbee*

"I used to volunteer at a local hospice. I did it for three years until I couldn't do it anymore. It was an incredible experience because when people know they are dying, so many of the barriers drop away and the opportunity to really get to know people exists. But then they died. In that short time, I became very close friends with five very different people, and they all died. I couldn't take it anymore.

"When I quit, I felt like such a failure. Here were all these people facing the most frightening thing imaginable, many of them completely alone in the world, and with all the wonderful things I have in my life I simply didn't have the heart to go on. For two years afterward I lived in a very small and protected world, feeling guilty the whole while. I didn't realize it then, but I needed my own time to heal, to process the painfully powerful feelings that had collected during my time at the hospice. I don't think I could work at a hospice again, but I feel the old need to reach out and connect with other people reemerging. Maybe this time I'll work with children."

We are people, not machines. We can't produce kindness and compassion endlessly at will, and it is not a failing to admit that. Our own lives, like everything around us, moves in cycles of action and reflection. Unfortunately, there is not a lot of support in this society for the reflection part of the cycle, which is one reason why so many people withdraw permanently into apathy.

What part of the cycle do you find yourself in today? Do you need to reach out or go in?

We need to have the wisdom to allow our lives to ebb and flow as they must, and the compassion not to judge ourselves harshly when we find ourselves in a place where our own needs overwhelm our capacity to give to others. Even the most beautiful flowers retreat with the coming of winter so that they might bring joy to our hearts the following spring.

Get Rid of Grudges

> "The grudge you hold on to is like a hot coal that you intend to throw at somebody else, but you're the one who gets burned."
>
> —The Buddha

"My neighbor's husband left her twenty years ago, and she refuses to get over it. I can't tell you how many times I have had to listen to her stories of what a complete jerk he was. The sad thing is that she is right; he was a jerk, and what he did and how he did it was mean, completely insensitive, and cruel. I know because he told me. He also told me that he tried to tell her the same thing many times, to acknowledge his wrongdoing and to seek her apology, but he finally gave up because she doesn't want to hear it. She thinks it's just him trying to be forgiven, and she isn't about to forgive him. The irony is that she thinks forgiveness will 'let him off the hook,' but she's the one that's still hooked. He remarried and is very happy, and she has been alone and bitter for twenty years."

We often think of forgiveness as something

we do for the other person, but forgiveness is really a kindness toward ourselves. For a grudge is a contraction of the heart, a holding ourselves back from positive feelings. When we hold a grudge, it stands in the way of love and kindness flowing into and out of our lives.

Is there someone you need to forgive? It could be for a tiny misdeed or an immense hurt. Forgiveness is not something that can be forced—it must come from an true expansion of spirit. One way to begin is to say that you are open to the possibility of forgiving. After you sit with that for as many days or weeks as it takes, you can progress to being willing to forgive, and then to forgiveness itself.

In order to bring more love into our lives, we need to practice forgiveness. It's a way of clearing the weeds in front of our hearts so that they can open and love can flow.

Make a Daily Difference

"We must not, in trying to think about how we can make a big difference, ignore the small daily differences we can make."
—*Marian Wright Edelman*

"The first time I ever saw him was by accident. There was a fender bender on the freeway, so I detoured through the city; as I drove down the road, I saw a old man standing on the sidewalk, waving. At first I couldn't tell who he was waving at, but as I drove by I realized that he was making eye contact with the driver of each car that went by and waving to all of us. It was so unusual it made me laugh. Then I found that almost without thinking, I had changed my route to work in the morning so I could go by the waving man. Pretty soon it was something I really looked forward to. He'd always be there waving, and more and more people—including myself— were waving back to him as we went by.

"This went on for years. Then on a few occasion he wouldn't be there, and I found myself worrying about him: Was he sick? Had something happened? Finally, after an unusually long absence, I read a story in the local paper that the waving man had grown too old and frail to weather his early-morning routine. It was like losing an old friend. I still drive by his spot and sometimes I wave at his house. I hope he knows how many morning smiles he was responsible for."

What gesture can you make that will make a difference? Like the waving man, it does not have to be big. The beauty of the practice of kindness is that it asks us to concentrate on what is right in front of our noses and to trust that, like the pebble in the pond, our tiny acts will ripple out into waves of positive change. We don't need to change the world; we need only to add those small acts of kindness that present themselves to us each day.

$\mathcal{L}$ove Your Precious Body

> "Making peace with your body, accepting it as it is, nurturing it with your care, feeding it well, nourishing it with exercise, admiring its beautiful aspects, honoring it with comfortable clothes, treating it as a temple, enjoying it as a ballroom, being awed by it as a palace—all these are expressions of kindness toward yourself."
> —*Daphne Rose Kingma*

Isn't it odd that we have such incredible difficulty coming to grips with the most basic and fundamental reality of our existence—our own body? At birth, we are given the gift of a most astonishingly miraculous organism, a human body. It will grow with us, enabling us to do, see, hear, smell, and feel the world we have inherited. It is totally unique, ours alone. It is the precious vessel for our mind, our heart, and our soul, and all too often we treat it with the most abject lack of respect. We abuse it, ignore it, obsess over all the parts we see as flawed. We often hate it for its size, shape, color, or texture and, in the most ungracious act of all, wish fervently that we had been given a different body—or at least some different parts.

If kindness indeed starts at home, certainly at the most basic level it must begin with an unswerving tenderness for and appreciation of our body. This is something that is often of particular difficulty for women. Because of the way society objectifies women's bodies and holds up certain types as ideal, it is quite easy for women to denigrate themselves physically, treating their bodies more ungraciously than they would any other living thing.

We can practice kindness toward our body by physically taking care of it and by refraining from negative self-talk, concentrating instead on how well it serves us. And we can extend that kindness to our friends. When we hear them complaining about their looks, we can gently and lovingly express our appreciation for their physical incarnation and our desire for them to treat their body with compassion.

$\mathcal{A}$cknowledge the Kindness of Others

> "No matter what accomplishments you achieve, somebody helps you."
> —Althea Gibson

"A few years back, I worked at an ad agency run by this very charismatic man. At first it was really exciting. He did a fantastic job of convincing us all that we were a team, and his cheerleading really kept us on our toes. Either he was very skilled at picking people or very lucky, because we were an incredibly creative and hardworking group and produced some pretty amazing work.

"The problems started surfacing when it became apparent to everyone on the so-called team that all our ideas, all our efforts, were being completely and totally expropriated by our boss. He took credit for everything, even to the point where he would stand there in the middle of client presentations and tell these elaborate lies about how he had come up with this or that concept. The cumulative effect was completely demoralizing.

Within a very short period, first the team effort and then the team itself simply dissolved. He managed to keep his company going for a few years, but eventually he ran out of good people who were willing to work for him. It struck me at the time that as good an administrator as he was, his fatal flaw was that he lacked the integrity to acknowledge the contribution of others."

Our culture is so immersed in individualism and competitiveness that it is easy to forget that nothing of lasting value is ever accomplished without the kind help of others. From the earliest support of our parents, teachers, and friends, to the supportive interaction of colleagues and the constant intellectual input of the ideas of authors, musicians, artists, and random strangers, we are helped along our path. Even the often difficult and painful lessons we stumble across in our lives are part of the assistance we receive.

Acknowledging the help we obtained—no matter what form it came in—will allow our hearts to soar like a well-tuned orchestra instead of a lonely violin. Today, give thanks to all the instruments in your life.

The Juice of Relationships

"Our relationships are kept moist and juicy by 'making love' all day long through conversation, presence, attention, and gentle kindness. Without dependable and meaningful connection between us, we dry up."

—*Sue Patton Thoele*

"I feel so lucky and so blessed. After fifty years of marriage, I look around me and see so few relationships that last with any fun, fire, and passion. So many times, people have asked us what our secret is, and I am always at a loss about how to respond. It has always been easy. I have heard my husband insist that he could never do enough to repay me for my kindness and understanding to him and it always amazes me, because I am just as convinced that it is I who can never do enough to repay him. If I had to explain the success of our relationship very simply, I guess I would have to say that we are very kind to each other, every day, and in every way possible."

So many people feel like they can fall in love

with someone, set up housekeeping, and then turn their attention to the rest of life, convinced that their relationship will run smoothly all on its own. Nothing could be further from the truth. The reality is, of course, that love requires a constant feeding from a stream of authentic presence and the responsive exchange of feelings and thoughts. It can survive neglect or bad feelings—for a while. But the soul of each of us is very tender and needs a great deal of loving attention from our spouse. In order to keep love alive, we need the balm of gentleness, the spice of appreciation, and the support of attention.

Above all, it needs kindness. Kindness is the magic elixir of love. It greases the rusty stuck places, fills up the frightful empty voids, dissolves the day's accumulated grime, smoothes the ruffled feathers, and fuels the fires of passion.

Seek Out a Kindness Angel

> "For those who dwell in the world and desire to embrace true virtue, it is necessary to unite themselves together by a holy and sacred friendship. By this means they encourage, assist, and conduct one another to good deeds."
> —*Saint Francis de Sales*

"Whenever I am out of sorts, scared, anxious, or angry, I always find myself calling this one particular friend. She listens so deeply and empathizes so completely that it never fails to soothe me. And her open-hearted position is not just reserved for close friends. Countless times, I have been with her in stores and taxi cabs, in small groups and large gatherings, and watched with amazement as she extends her understanding and compassion to everyone around her. Lately, I've begun to notice that just being around her has had a dramatic impact on my own behavior. Where once I might have rushed to make a judgment, I find myself listening more intently. Where once I might have just said some social thing, now I find myself imagining what this person's circumstance must feel like and saying something that is more from the heart. Suddenly people are gathering around me, too."

Our attitudes and actions are, to a greater or lesser degree, shaped by those around us. We see this all the time with kids, particularly teens. But it's true for adults as well. If we spend a lot of time with negative people who think the world is going to hell in a handbasket, it's likely we too will see only the bad in the world. If we seek out the angels in our midst, we are not only reminded of the power and rewards of compassion, but we gain valuable insight into how to act in a loving manner.

By associating with people who are committed to doing good deeds, you will find it easier to do so also.

Teach Kindness to Kids

"As adults, we must ask more of our children than they know how to ask of themselves. What can we do to foster their open-hearted hopefulness, engage their need to collaborate, be an incentive to utilize their natural competency and compassion . . . show them ways they can connect, reach out, weave themselves into the web of relationships that is called community?"

—*Dawna Markova*

"A friend of mine works with a group that tries to provide alternative avenues and models for children who have been in trouble with the law. I am always surprised by the distance between the kids she talks about and the anonymous 'juvenile delinquents' the newspapers are always warning us about. The twisted, amoral, little monsters of the morning paper turn into the scared, wounded, desperate children in my afternoon conversation with Sheila. When I commented on this to her once, she told me that, contrary to what many parents believe, children actually do pretty much what they are taught to do.

*"These kids were just taught,' she explained, 'unfortunately by how they were treated, to see the world as a cruel and brutal fight for survival, and it has taken a terrible toll on their lives. All we try to do is show them by example, by how we act toward them and among ourselves, that it's not true, that there is a world out there of people willing to join hands and help one another."

So if you want to teach your children well, be a model of kindness and compassion. Treat them and their friends kindly. Let the example you set be one of understanding and generosity. Invite them to participate with you in finding new ways to inject more kindness into the world.

If our mail is any indication (we've received thousands of letters from kids about random acts of kindness), kids are kindness junkies once they are shown the way. Make an investment in their future by showing them how to help bring about a gentler and more compassionate world.

Take Quiet Time

> "Only when one is connected to one's own core is one connected to others. And, for me, the core, the inner spring, can best be re-found through solitude."
> —*Anne Morrow Lindberg*

"I do it to myself all the time even though I know better. I know that for me to be a decent functioning human being, I need time to myself. For me, just as my body needs sleep to rest and recuperate, my mind needs silence to let me sink back into myself. Yet without my even noticing, my schedule starts filling up and then speeding up until I am so wound up I'm operating on nothing but nervous energy. When I get into those states, I'm not fun to be around. I snap and growl, I'm impatient with everything and everyone, and I completely lose track of everything that is important to me.

"The hardest part of this for me is being able to tell when I've crossed the line. It is almost like the world is constantly sucking us into a more and more frenetic pace. I finally decided I just had to schedule down time; I couldn't rely on myself to do it when I needed it. So now, every two weeks I take an entire afternoon and escape. Sometimes to the hills behind my house, sometimes to wonderfully deserted beaches, and sometimes just behind the closed door of my room. The effect is always amazing. When I return, I see things so clearly and, most important, feel things so solidly. Then I can really be there for everyone else."

When was the last time you were alone? For how long? Give yourself the gift of solitude so that you will always be ready to offer the world the gift of your heart.

$\mathcal{L}$isten as an Act of Kindness

> "When one's own problems are unsolvable and all best efforts are frustrated, it is lifesaving to listen to other people's problems."
>
> —*Suzanne Massie*

"I was having coffee with a friend one day and sat there, hunched over my cup, preoccupied with a long list of problems that seemed unresolvable. Suddenly my friend said, 'You haven't heard a thing I've said,' and to my complete embarrassment I realized it was true. I stood up, shook my whole body, sat down, took a few deep breaths and said, 'Okay, I'm really sorry. I'm listening now.'

"It was kind of a joke, but it worked. I suddenly found it very easy to be really focused on what she was saying. We talked for a while longer, and when I left, I realized that for some reason, just listening, really listening, and responding to her tale of woes had made *me* feel so much better. My problems were still there, but they didn't seem so urgent anymore. I knew that her being able to really share what was going on in her life had helped her as well. Nothing really had changed, but in some strange way, on some deeper level, everything had changed."

As this story shows, deep listening is an act of kindness not only to the other person but also to ourselves. It takes us out of our self-focus to offer empathy to the other person, and at the same time reminds us we are not alone in our suffering. When we listen well, we are able to both offer solace, companionship, and support, and at the same time to remember that we are really a part of a much larger community.

Today, take the opportunity to truly listen to someone, if only for a brief time. What happens to you?

Stay Balanced

> "Giving and receiving should be practiced alternately."
>
> —*Geshe Chekhawa*

"When I was growing up, my parents had a thing about dinner. Everyone took turns participating in meal preparation, and we always ate together in the evening. When everyone was seated, one of the meal preparers would stand up, look each of us in the eye, and say, 'I offer you this nourishment in appreciation of all you give to me.' At times, it felt really hokey, often getting wildly funny when we would improvise with the offering; and sometimes, like the first time my brother fixed dinner after getting back from the hospital after a serious biking accident, it was very emotional. Mostly, it made us feel close to each other. It was a ritual of closeness built upon a constant cycle of giving and receiving, reminding us every day how much we got from each other and how wonderful it was to be able to give in return."

In many ways, our whole lives can be

viewed as a continuous cycle of transaction, receiving gifts from others—love, wisdom, lessons, support, and kindness—pausing to appreciate what we have received, perhaps polishing those gifts that are slightly tarnished, and then passing them on to other recipients. This is, in a profound and basic way, the essence of the web of life. All of creation, from the tiniest particle to the greatest mountain, is involved in an ongoing exchange of energy.

In seeking to perfect our small part in this magical exchange, we need to make sure that we stay in balance. How balanced are you in terms of this beautiful dance of life? Are you receiving what you need so that what you pass on to others will sparkle like diamonds and reflect the deepest parts of your heart? If not, what can you do to correct the imbalance?

Discover Your Delights

> "When we lack proper time for the simple pleasures of life, for the enjoyment of eating, drinking, playing, creating, visiting friends, and watching children at play, then we have missed the purpose of life. Not on bread alone do we live but on all these human and heart-hungry luxuries."
>
> —*Ed Hays*

"When I was seven, my father was working long hours on some project at his job, and as time went by he was getting more and more cranky. He'd bite our head off and then apologize a few minutes later. When he finally finished what he was working on, he promised my sister and me that he'd spend the whole day with us on Saturday. But my mother pulled us both aside and told us that what Dad really needed right then was something that would recharge his batteries. So we came up with a secret plan, and on Saturday morning, all three of us snuck into the kitchen and made up a big breakfast and served it to him in bed. Then when he had showered and got dressed, we were all lined up in the living room with his golf clubs between us.

"At first he tried to beg off, telling us he really appreciated the gesture but he wanted to spend the day with us like he had promised. But my little sister, proving that even at age five she had understood what Mom meant, told him, 'We'd rather spend time with you later when you're charged up.' I'll always remember how happy he was that day."

We all have so many demands on our time. It's virtually impossible to get everything done that we *have* to do, much less that which we *want* to do. But if we go too long without time to enjoy the simple, unique pleasures of our lives, life becomes sheer drudgery, and happiness goes out the window.

What are the little things that make your heart sing and lighten your load? For one person, it is sitting in hot water for ten minutes; for someone else, it is watching koi swim in a pond. If you don't tap into those things on a regular basis, you can't be available to be loving or kind to anyone else. Make time in your life for the things that recharge your batteries, for the things that make you smile and bring you joy. Everyone will benefit.

$\mathcal{P}$*ractice* Is the Operative Word

> "Like a wish or a work of art, the beauty of love is sculpted over time. The love you imagine and desire will become yours only through a constancy of effort."
> —Daphne Rose Kingma

All of what we want in life takes effort—and that includes intangibles such as love, happiness, and serenity, as well as things like a Porsche or a strong body. Although we want to believe that once is enough, that all good things will come to us, the truth is that constancy is required: remembering daily to do the considerate thing, offer the encouraging word, take the moment of solitude for oneself. Our children and spouse need to hear every day that we love them; we need the space every day to replenish and renew ourselves.

This is why the practice of loving-kindness is just that—*practice*. Like a figure skater learning a jump, you have to do it over and over again. Sometimes you'll do it better than the time before; other times you'll fall flat on your fanny. Sometimes it feels great, as if you are in the groove and can do no wrong; other times you have to do it kicking and screaming the whole way. But you put the time in no matter what, hour after hour, day after day.

The good news is that it is never too late to start or to restart when we forget, as we inevitably will. And the better news is that when it comes to cultivating kindness, practice *does* makes perfect. The more we do it, the better we get—and the more we get back.

Kindness
Ripples out
into the World

"What we do today, right now, will have an accumulated effect on all our tomorrows."
—Alexandra Stoddard

$\mathcal{W}$e live in a crowded and tumultuous time, so bursting with noise that just to take notice of the world threatens to overwhelm us. We long for a simpler, quieter time, a time of small villages, peaceful valleys, and pastures full of the sounds of nature instead of the blaring of horns, screeching of tires, and constant background din of internal combustion engines. In our mythology, our legends, our fairy tales, the world is always small enough to embrace, small enough that we can see the purpose of our being there, follow the threads of our lives, and know that what we do has a lasting effect.

But that time has gone and is not likely to return. We have been born into a world teeming with souls and echoing with the noise of discord, and it is our task to learn how to effectively be ourselves in the midst of that seeming chaos. Often, the most difficult part of that task is simply being able to see or sense the threads that connect us, that bind us together, the invisible arteries through which our actions pulse and flow out into the community of others.

We need to hone our deeper sense of connectedness. Learning to master this sixth sense is not unlike how as children we learned to use our first five senses—we experiment, we extend ourselves outward, feeling for the ways and places that we are connected, opening channels of kindness and understanding, and watching them ripple outward. In this section, the practices focus on ways to explore, strengthen, and expand those connections.

ℒook to Your Neighborhood

> "So many people say they want to save
> the world. Just try your block, will you?"
> —*Rev. Cecil Williams*

"It started five years ago as a neighborhood protection society after a couple of houses were broken into. We went to meetings, had the police come by and give us anti-burglary tips, put up 'Neighborhood Watch' stickers in the windows, and worried about what was happening to our nice, quiet neighborhood.

"When we found out that the burglars were kids on our block, everything changed. At first there was a lot of anger and blaming, but I was surprised at how quickly that changed. We started meeting to talk about how different it was for kids today compared to when we were growing up, and we realized that for most of the kids in our area, there was nothing to do and nowhere to play.

"So we put our heads and our backs together and last week we inaugurated our very own 'pocket park.' It has a recreational center and an odd-sized but useable playing field. It took a lot of time and hard work and was meant for the kids, but by the turnout and smiles at our 'parkwarming,' it meant as much to the adults as the kids."

Many of us think readily of kind acts when we think about those closest to us—our family and friends—and those farthest away—those starving in Somalia or dying in Bosnia. But sometimes the hardest place to keep in mind is our own neighborhood.

Sometimes we don't even have a notion of what our community is. What is your sense of your neighborhood? How many streets does it encompass? Is it just the four houses around you? Do you know your neighbors? Do you know your neighborhood's needs and concerns? Today, just notice your relationship to your neighborhood.

$\mathcal{F}$ocus on the Particular

"When I look at the world, I'm pessimistic.
But when I look at people, I'm optimistic."
—*Carl Rogers*

It's easy to make negative generalizations about groups of people. A friend of ours was given a great lesson about this by his son Tim last year. Tim had cut school and was spotted by his father, wandering around downtown with a couple of friends. That night his dad lowered the boom and told Tim he was not to hang around "those purple-haired freaks" anymore (one of his truant friends was a young woman sporting the latest in teen fashion—purple hair and an earring in her nose).

Tim responded that he deserved to be punished but that his father was way off base blaming his friends for his misbehavior. Tim told his dad that he ought to at least give him credit for making his own stupid decisions; his friends were not skipping school—their classes were over. Besides, hadn't he always taught Tim that it wasn't right to judge people you don't even know? His dad calmed down a bit, saw that Tim was making more sense than he was, and relented. As time went on, the purple-haired friend (since returned to natural blonde) became a good friend of the whole family and baby-sits their smallest child every week.

Generalizations kill kindness. When we look at someone as a representative of a group, say, "the homeless," it's easy to make hurtful assumptions and look upon them as something less than human. But if we take the time to look at the particular individual—the homeless woman on the street with the little dog—we can see her humanity and it is more difficult to be unkind.

Not making generalizations has another benefit. By focusing on the individual, we can see our potential efficacy. We may not be able to help "the homeless" in general, but perhaps we can help this one woman find shelter. If we focus on the broad generalizations, we are doomed to despair. By focusing on who and what is right in front of us, we can build connections and make a small, but effective, difference.

ℐhe Kindness of Nature

> "When you walk across the fields with your mind pure and holy, then from all the stones, and all growing things, and all animals, the sparks of their soul come out and cling to you, and then they are purified and become a holy fire in you."
>
> —*Hasidic saying*

"When I was younger, I hiked up into the Himalayas for three weeks. It was an absolutely incredible experience. I remember walking through those majestic mountains, captivated by everything I saw. I was surrounded by so much beauty I was suffering from sensory overload. I would walk a little and then just stop trying to take it all in. Sixty-foot-tall Rhododendron trees, eight-inch-wide blossoms floating down gurgling pure mountain creeks, expansive vistas reaching up to the highest peaks in the world—it was like wandering through a fairy-tale land where each corner turned revealed a land more stunning and beautiful.

"Later, when I was back home, I was walking one day across the field behind my parents house and something of that same experience came back to me. As I looked around at the twisted oaks and listened to the birds calling to each other, I realized that as truly magnificent as the Himalayas are, it was only the new and exotic nature of the scenery that opened my eyes. I could see that everywhere—from the flower gardens on a suburban street to the horizon-to-horizon wheat fields of the Midwest to the craggy seashore of New England—was a world of extraordinary vibrancy and grace."

We are born into a world that is rich with beauty. It is there for us at every moment at every turn, to replenish our hearts, to rekindle our enthusiasm, to remind us of how much we have to be grateful for. The world itself is a deep well of kindness from which we can draw. So walk through it with open eyes and an open heart, and it will fill you to overflowing.

We Need One Another

> "No one is rich enough to do without a neighbor."
>
> —*Danish proverb*

We read a story in the newspaper the other day that really upset us. A man working for the electric company had gone out to a wealthy home to turn off the power (the bill had not been paid) and discovered a dead body. It turned out to be the woman who had lived there. She had apparently fallen and broken her hip and was unable to move. God only knows how long she lay there before she died, but the police estimated that she had died nearly three months before her body was discovered. All we could think was, How could someone be so alone in the world that they could disappear without a trace for three months without anyone noticing?

Stories like this are commonplace nowadays. So many of us seem to have lost connection to everyone and everything. One of the reasons seems to be that in these days of high-speed electronic information delivery, we are bombarded with news of every horrible thing, and our first reaction is often to retreat. We remove ourselves from our community, build higher walls, install stronger security devices, and are afraid to go out and speak to those around us.

Yet withdrawal from the world not only leaves us lonely and isolated from the comfort of community, but is also a tragic illusion. Our most sacred nature is that we are a society of people, not merely a smattering of individuals. We need each other, and when we try to retreat we are only fooling ourselves. We need each other—to grow, transport and deliver our food, build and maintain our means of communication, teach and tend our children, heal our bodies, and accomplish the thousands of other tasks that directly or indirectly support our lives.

Remembering this complex and necessary interdependence can remind us of the daily assistance we receive from thousands of strangers and can make it that much easier for us to return our kindness to the pool.

$\mathcal{L}$ook in
Surprising Places

"I made connection with a pair of eyes, and thought, 'This is incredible; these eyes are penetrating me.' I went through the whole performance just relating to those eyes, giving the whole thing to those eyes. When curtain call finally came, I looked in the directions of those eyes, and it was a seeing-eye dog. . . . I couldn't get over it—the compassion and intensity and understanding in those eyes, and it was a dog."

—Al Pacino, *about a theatrical performance*

"One of the first things I noticed when we moved into our new home was the birds. Every morning I woke up to the beautiful sound of birds calling out their morning song. It was almost a year before I realized that their presence was really a gift from my neighbor, who had an elaborate bird feeder set up in her backyard just a few feet away from my bedroom window. She died this past year, and the people who moved in never kept up the bird feeder.

"One day when I woke up, I felt surrounded

by a cloud of sadness. I lay there for a while, trying to figure out what was causing it and finally realized it was because my morning symphony had flown. I turned toward my husband lying next to me, and he said, 'It's the birds, they're gone.' That day we went to the store and bought a spectacular bird feeder and set it up in the backyard. Our morning friends are back now."

The things that nourish us, give us joy, and help us to live in our hearts take many forms. Humans are so self-focused that it's easy to see people as the source and purpose of everything and forget that we are only a part of this miracle of creation. But truly "creature kindness" is around each and every one of us.

Take a little time right now to notice and be thankful for the comfort and support you are given each day by the animals that surround you. And take care and act kindly toward all our companions in this journey.

To Know God, Love Thy Neighbor

> "If anyone says, 'I love God,' and hates his brother, he is a liar; for he who does not love his brother whom he has seen, cannot love God whom he has not seen."
> —*Jesus Christ*, 1 John 4:21

"Many years ago, there was an old man in our town who used to irritate everyone. He walked around with a Bible under his arm, always ready to spout scripture, but he was the most angry, unfriendly person. One of his favorite targets was homosexuals. He'd stand outside the local gay coffee shop, castigating everyone who went in or out.

"At some point, it became obvious that he was really sick, and it turned out he had gotten AIDS from a blood transfusion. At that time, the only people who were really doing outreach and support for AIDS patients were the gay community. Even though they knew him well from the years of abuse, they took him under their wing. At first, he was incredibly ungrateful and abusive, but as his body weakened, he lost some of his old anger. He spent the last months of his life in a hospice surrounded by gay men. They were his only support and his only comfort, and when he died, they were his only friends."

It is a basic tenet of every religion that each of us, even the most bitter and narrow-minded, carries within a spark of the divine. It's easy to be loving in the abstract, but not always so easy to actually be kind to those who cross our path. How many people do you know who love God but seem to have such contempt for the individuals around them? In truth, as this quote reminds us, it is only by being loving to those around us that we learn to love God.

$\mathcal{K}$indness Toward Difficult People

> "Love means to love that which is unlovable; or it is no virtue at all."
> —G. K. Chesterton

Some acts of kindness are relatively easy—stopping to help an elderly woman fix a tire on a day you aren't in a hurry, for example. Others, such as volunteering your time to a community group on a regular basis, are much more difficult. But few are as tough as offering compassion to someone you dislike. So often we want to be nice only to those whom we feel are worthy—the mate who brings us roses, the friend who always has a cheery word. But what about the sour-faced person in the cubicle next to you? Perhaps her husband has been laid off and she's terrified about money. Perhaps she's been trying to get pregnant for five years and is in despair over never having a child. By simply being alive, she is as deserving of kindness as anyone else.

We may never *like* that coworker or the

seemingly nosy next-door neighbor, but we can and should act graciously toward them nonetheless. We don't even need to know what makes them crabby or nosy to extend our goodwill. When we offer our kindness to even those who don't seem "deserving" of it, we are developing our capacity to love impersonally, what the Greeks called *agape*.

True kindness is not a reward to be handed out only to those who have earned it; rather, it is a way for us to reconnect with our own humanity. Through kindness, we are reminded that we are all family and that even the black sheep need to be included in the comfort and support of the fold.

Honor the Earth That Gives Us Life

> "Remember, remember the sacredness of things / running streams and dwellings / the young within the nest / a hearth for sacred fire / the holy flame."
>
> —*Omaha Indian chant*

"I had been in a fog for weeks. I was grouchy, out of sorts; my mind was skipping from one thing to another, seemingly without any reason or purpose, and I was filled with a building anxiety, like I was forgetting something important or, worse, that something bad was about to happen if I didn't figure out quickly what was going on.

"Then one morning, I woke up feeling the same and discovered it was also foggy outside. I looked out the window and realized that the fog was putting on an amazing display. First, it would move in with great swirls, blocking out the sky and surrounding everything until I couldn't see down the street. Then, it would sneak back out like a tide and reveal a brilliant blue sky. Then it would sink down to ground level, leaving the tops of houses exposed to the bright sun, while wrapping pedestrians in blankets of mist so thick it looked like a movie set.

"Instead of doing the work I had planned, I ended up watching the fog all morning. By the afternoon, it burned off and I found myself sad to see it go. Suddenly my own fog, the one that I had carried around in my head for so long, also dissipated in the shining afternoon sun. I laughed in delight at the amazing ways the world has of delivering its messages."

We live in a wonderland of beauty and mystery. The more we hone our skills of observation and develop our sense of connectedness to all that surrounds us, the greater and deeper the wealth of experience of peace, joy, and beauty that is available to us.

Today, take the time to feel the air on your face, to marvel at the majesty of weather. Feel yourself a part of the extraordinary nature of our world, and let it fill you with its blessing.

Be Extravagant with Yourself

> "I fear chiefly lest my expression may not be extra-vagant, may not wander far beyond the narrow limits of my daily experience, so as to be adequate to the truth of which I have been convinced. Extra-vagant! It depends on how you are yarded."
> —*Henry David Thoreau*

"One summer when my brother and I were still in high school, we were lying on the front lawn, bored silly, and he said, 'You know, old lady Henderson sure has let her yard go.' Right there, we hatched a plan to make a midnight gardening raid. The next day, Mrs. Henderson was standing out in her yard, talking about how some elves had transformed her overgrown garden into neatly trimmed bushes. "It was so much fun that we planned a raid on another neighbor's yard a few days later. When the sun rose the day after, the hedge around the yard across the street was all trimmed. My mother must have figured out it was us, because later that day she made some comment about how the corner lot sure would look better with some flowers along the sidewalk instead of that bare patch of dirt, and later that afternoon we discovered four flats of flowers sitting in our garage just waiting for the midnight raiders.

"It was great fun, and we lasted almost a month before we finally got caught—there is just no way to mow lawn silently. It not only brought smiles to the entire neighborhood, but people started taking better care of their yards, and we even ended up getting some gardening jobs."

As we grow up, we unconsciously accept boundaries for our lives—our home, our family, our friends, our neighborhood, our country. These boundaries give us an identity, but they can also hold us back from the fullness of life, aching to be expressed through us.

When it comes to exercising our hearts, it is important not to let unconscious fences hold us back. Constrained, restrained expressions of kindness are no fun compared to what an exuberant unbounded heart can dream up if it is allowed to expand into the world with as much enthusiasm as possible. What kind, grand gesture can you think up?

The Temple of Community

> "Suppose you considered your neighborhood to be your temple—how would you treat your temple and what would your spiritual task be there?"
>
> —Jack Kornfield

"As an adult, I used to hate Halloween because my childhood memories of it were so great, and it seemed that the spirit had been lost. Nobody on our street would even put out jack-o'lanterns, and I'd have to drive the kids halfway across town to find a few houses where they could go trick-or-treating.

"Then a few years ago, a couple moved in across from me, and on Halloween their whole front yard had magically transformed itself into yard of horrors. It so captivated everyone that the next year, half the houses on the street had made at least some effort to dress up for the evening. This past year was the best of all. Virtually every single house was decorated with jack-o'lanterns, scary music filled the night air, and excited kids ran from house to house, squealing in delight. What was most amazing was that all night long, roving bands of smiling parents were meeting up on the sidewalks and joining in on the fun."

Whether it is tending a beautiful flower garden, throwing an occasional party just for the neighbors, cleaning up the eyesores on your property, going out of your way to greet people, or finding your own way to contribute to a sense of community—treating your neighborhood as a temple is the first step toward making the world a sacred vessel for our souls. What one tiny thing can you do to enhance your community?

Take a Lesson from the Mosquito

> "If you think you are too small to be effective, you have never been in bed with a mosquito."
>
> —*Betty Reese*

"I was a transcription secretary in a large eastern city before I retired, and one of my weekly functions was to record the city council meetings. Very early on, I began to notice that every week during the public-input portion of the meeting, this very polite woman would go up to the podium and talk about the desperate need for recreational opportunities for inner-city kids and then return to her seat. She would also send a letter on the subject to every council member each week—sometimes with stories of how kids tried to compensate for the absence of opportunities, sometimes just passionate pleas, occasionally with newspaper clippings about the tragic things that were happening to those kids.

"Now I have to tell you that budgeting

money for inner-city recreation was very low on the priority list. But year after year, she kept coming and kept writing. Pretty soon, I noticed that the council members were greeting her in the hall almost as an old friend. Nothing miraculous happened but, gradually, the budget for the recreation department began to grow. Even in years when other departments were being cut, somehow the council was convinced that the recreation department had a particularly compelling project in midstream, and its budget would increase marginally. She kept that up for almost ten years, and in many ways was the most effective advocate I ever saw appear before the council."

The problems of the world are so immense that it's very easy to feel that nothing we can do will help. But like the recreation lady, with the impact of the mosquito and the perseverance of the ant, we can slowly but deliberately transform a tiny corner of the world. Just remember: We don't need to solve the world's problems today—we need only take one small step in that direction.

Recall the Kindness of Strangers

"They have been men whose names are unknown because they cared little for fame, and truth radiated from them without their knowing it. They have been revealers who were unaware of the revelation that was in them; modest sages that mingled their wisdom with their daily life. . . . We have all met, at least once in our lives, one of these unheralded initiators, and received from them a priceless gift, by a kindly word, a . . . sincere expression in the eyes."

—*Maurice Magre*

When we were compiling the *Random Acts of Kindness* series, we received thousands of letters from people, mostly telling us of the incredible acts of kindness they had been recipients of—meals when they were hungry, beds to sleep in when they were lost, support and understanding when they were ready to despair. But we received very few letters about good deeds that folks had done themselves. At first, we believed that people were just modest, that they didn't want to toot their own horn.

But as time went on, we came to see that it was not humility that held people back. It was because a kind act, no matter the size, is much more significant to the recipient than it is to the giver. The twenty-five cents you drop in the parking meter means virtually nothing to you, but to the financially struggling student who avoided a twenty-dollar parking ticket, it is a very big deal. The directions you give to a scared older woman in the city may take you only thirty seconds, but they save her an hour of panic. As givers, we simply do what seems right at the moment, but to the receiver, such deeds are often life-savers.

In practicing kindness, it's crucially important to remember the times people were helpful or considerate to you, or brought a moment of unexpected joy into your life. It is a constant reminder that the vast array of small kindness opportunities that present themselves to you each day could be extremely meaningful to those around you.

Walk a Mile in the Other Person's Shoes

> "If we could read the secret history of our enemies, we should find, in each man's life, sorrow and suffering enough to disarm all hostility."
>
> —Henry Wadsworth Longfellow

"When I was in college, there was a guy in my dorm who was the most perfect jerk imaginable. Everything he did seemed especially crafted to irritate everyone around him. He'd toss cynical comments into other people's conversations, wander around in a calculated state of slovenliness, and leave a trail of slop and mess behind him. It seemed his goal in life was to make everyone hate him—and he was doing a good job of it. Toward the end of the first semester, we had parents' day at the dorm, and was that ever an eye-opener! This guy's father was something else—sort of a cross between a Marine drill sergeant and Archie Bunker with a really loud, booming voice. Suddenly, I could understand why he might be acting the way he was, and though we never became close, at least I could be nicer to him."

We can cultivate feelings of compassion to those who annoy, anger, or upset us by remembering that we are all wounded and that some of us are less skillful than others in dealing with it. One way to do this is to assume that the person who is driving us crazy has good reason to be grouchy, inconsiderate, or plain mean.

When we look through the eyes of compassion, we can at least open a place for understanding to grow, to know that something in their past—a history of abuse, neglect, abandonment, or depravation—might well have pushed them toward this place. We need not approve of their behavior or agree with their choices, but we can empathize with the suffering they must have endured to get there, and hold open the possibility of their healing. In so doing, we bring compassion into their lives—and into our own.

Remember We're in This Together

> "The only justification for ever looking down on somebody is to pick them up."
> —*The Reverend Jesse Jackson*

"I was returning home on a flight from the East Coast after burying my father. It had been a very difficult time. I had known Dad was sick for some time, but my own anxiety about illness and death had me twisted in knots—I kept putting off visiting him until it was too late. All I wanted was to be left alone to my thoughts. So of course I ended up on a full flight, sitting next to a man about my age, who obviously wanted to talk.

"At first I resisted his attempts to get a conversation going, giving one-word answers, looking like I was really interested in my inflight magazine. But it was useless. Then he told me very matter-of-factly that he was on his way home to die. I guess I kind of recoiled at that, so he said, 'Don't worry, it isn't contagious.' Somewhat to my own amazement, I heard the words 'Are you scared?' come flying out of my mouth. Normally, I would never have been so direct, but my own experience had really affected me. Anyway, that certainly broke the ice, and we ended up deep in conversation throughout the entire flight.

"It was such a liberating experience for me. This guy was no hero and no saint. He was scared, he was confused, he was angry, he was worried about how he would handle dying, and he was afraid his whole life had meant nothing; but through it all, he was determined to at least face what was happening to him as honestly and courageously as possible, and in some small way I felt honored to be able to participate."

It is so easy to become preoccupied with ourselves as lone individuals. After all, it is what our physical senses report to us. But we are not alone—we are just one of many, all struggling with the same issues, all trying to move in the same direction. We need each other for the deepest spiritual reasons. We need each other to share the mysteries of life and death, to give substance to our joy and sorrows, to help us on our journey, and to remind us that we are all one.

Take Time to Savor Life

"Life is so short we must move very slowly."

—*Thai proverb*

"The last time I visited France, I took one of the new trains—the pride of the French rail service—the TGV (which is the French acronym for "really fast train") from Paris to Lyon. I must admit, it was very fast and in its own way very impressive, but I came away from the whole experience with a lingering sense of sadness. The grand old train stations in Paris have all been remodeled to accommodate the new trains, and, strangely, the kind of elegantly contained and relaxed bustle that used to characterize the stations has been replaced by a very stripped-down efficiency. It just felt like somehow we had thrown out all the character and charm for the sake of a marginal increase in efficiency.

"Once you got on the train, the difference was even more dramatic and disturbing. To this day, some of the most powerful memories I have are scenes of the French countryside slipping by from the window of a train. But you can't even look out from the windows of the TGV without getting an instant headache. You are moving so fast that it is impossible to bring any of the passing countryside into focus—it is simply a blur."

When we are rushed, we can easily lose sight of the preciousness of life. When we go too fast, we do ourselves a great unkindness, for we are not available to the beauty and grace around us—the golden butterfly floating across our path, the great blue heron perched by the side of the road, the sound of the wind through the aspens, the sight of an old church spire rising up out of a small village.

These are all gratuitous gifts, uncounted blessings that are offered to us each day, random acts of beauty just waiting to be noticed. Life is indeed too short and too precious to race through without noticing. Slow down today and savor the surprising wealth you discover.

Don't Overlook Sharing

> "Sharing is something more demanding
> than giving."
> —*Mary Catherine Bateson*

"When my parents died, they left the five of us kids a beautiful cabin high up in the mountains. Sharing it has been a fascinating experience. At first, it was a first-come, first-served kind of reservation system. But then one of my sisters complained that she hardly ever used it and that my two brothers used it all the time, so when she *did* want to use it, there should be some way to account for that. Then, of course, there were the cleaning and repairing issues: Someone would break something and not replace it, and then there would be a tracking down of the wrongdoer by a resentful sibling forced to rectify the situation on his or her vacation time.

"I guess I was surprised at how difficult it was to share even with your own family. At times, things have gotten strained enough that we tentatively begin talking about whether we should sell the cabin. But last

Christmas we all got together—the first time since our parents died—and at some point ended up talking about the cabin, about how beautiful the morning light was coming in the window over the sink, about how every time any of us went there we could always feel the comforting presence of our parents. We decided that the cabin was something we wanted to share, no matter how difficult it got sometimes, just as we had shared our parents for so many years."

Sharing provides many opportunities to learn about ourselves and our capacity for kindness. It allows us to offer our resources to others and to be aided in return, and to see how possessive, self-righteous, or uncooperative we might be. Sharing also is a way for us to treat the world more gently, by avoiding the mindless accumulation of material things. Despite the insistence of well-crafted commercials, we do not all need the latest toys. One lawn mower can service many lawns; one cabin can shelter many families.

When we choose to share something, we stretch our souls and spare the earth—at least a little.

$\mathcal{T}$he Power of a Tiny Act

> "'Who are you really, wanderer?' and the answer you have to give is: 'Maybe I am a king.'"
>
> —William Stafford

Here's an apocryphal story we heard while writing *Random Acts of Kindness*. Is it true? It only matters that it could be.

One day in Los Angeles, a hot dog vendor, pressed by a personal emergency, turned to a homeless man and asked him to watch over his stand while he left to take care of his crisis. Hours passed. When the vendor returned, he paid the man for his time and thanked him for tending the stand. Years later, the homeless man came back, this time dressed in a business suit, and told the vendor that he was now a millionaire. "Because you gave me a chance," he said, "because you trusted me, I was able to believe in myself and turn my life around."

Life works in mysterious ways. People flow in and out of our lives like leaves floating down a river. We can see each arrival and departure as unconnected, random events, or we can search within them for a subtle, guiding hand and seize on them as opportunities. What am I being called to do at this moment? What can I learn from this situation? What can I offer that will help this person on their journey through life?

Each chance encounter offers us the opportunity to choose to make a difference in the world. And each choice we make, small as it may seem, might be the grain that tipped the balance or the thread that finally tied the knot for someone. Choose courageously and generously, for each act of kindness ripples out into the world with pure potential.

ℒife Is Loving Us

> "There is in all things an inexhaustible sweetness and purity, a silence that is a fountain of action and joy. It rises up in wordless gentleness and flows out to me from unseen roots of all created being."
> —*Thomas Merton*

"When my girlfriend broke up with me, she said she just couldn't take my negative attitude anymore. 'All you see is what's wrong,' she said, and sadly I knew she was right. I brooded about it for a while—brooding was something that came naturally to me—and came up with what I thought was a pretty lame plan: For one week I was going to write down every good thing that I saw or experienced.

"It took a few days to get into the swing of it, but then something amazing happened: I actually started finding more and more things. It was almost as if the world was responding to my efforts—an old friend called out of the blue, my grumpy physics professor complimented me in class, people all around me were smiling at me and including me in conversations, I found a book I thought I had lost, even the weather suddenly turned spectacular. The list went on and on for four pages. I know it sounds weird, but I am convinced that something out there was responding to my being willing to keep track of the good things."

It seems that one of the most fundamental characteristics of humans is our capacity to lose track of the good around us and see only the bad. Gifted through the miracle of creation with a marvelous mind to think, reflect, and analyze, we all too easily get lost in our own private world and ignore the amazing web of life that supports us and caresses us on a daily basis.

As you go about your day today, try keeping your mind and heart open so that you will see and feel all the ways in which the world around us offers the benedictions of a loving friend.

The Grand Show

> "The grand show is eternal. It is always
> sunrise somewhere; the dew is never
> dried all at once; a shower is forever fall-
> ing; vapor is ever rising. Eternal sunrise,
> eternal dawn and gloaming, on sea and
> continents and islands, each in its turn,
> as the round earth rolls."
>
> —John Muir

"I read a science-fiction book a while back
that wasn't very well written, but one piece
of it keeps coming back to me. In the book,
the sprawl of humanity had so fouled the
earth that all the birds died off. I can't get
that picture out of my mind—the idea of
standing in a field or at the ocean, walking
through an orchard or a forest, and hearing
only silence where songs of birds should be.
How devastatingly sad a place the world
would be without birds! Then I am forced to
remember that this is not so far removed
from where we are today. Every year, thousands of living species crowded out of their
niches die and are gone forever."

As a species, we suffer from the same

shortsightedness we struggle with as individuals—only the consequences are so dramatically magnified. Our preoccupation with ourselves, and our difficulty seeing ourselves as a part of a much larger picture, has led us down a trail of squandering and abuse of the riches that make up our planet.

As individuals who wish to bring more kindness, love, and compassion into the world, it is time for us to step back and see clearly our place in the grand show of creation so that we may act our part respectfully and appropriately. We are unique among all the creatures and organisms of this world. And the very qualities that make us unique dictate for us the sacred role of stewards of creation. In our ignorance and conceit, however, we have interpreted that extraordinary gift as permission to blindly plunder for our own most narrow and immediate purposes.

Each of us can begin to take our responsibility seriously. We *can* act the part of a caring steward to all of creation and never lose track of our place in the grand show.

Connection to the All

"If you are unfaithfully here, you are causing great damage. But if your love is joined
to the great Love, you are helping people
you don't know and have never met."

—Rumi

There have been numerous articles and
books recently about a series of studies on
the effect of prayer on healing. Groups of
patients with a similar condition and prog-
nosis were identified, and volunteers were
instructed to pray on a regular basis and in
whatever manner they wanted for some randomly selected sick individuals. None of the
patients knew they were being prayed for. In
study after study, those who were prayed for
did better—often remarkably better—than
those who received no prayers. They also
found that proximity was irrelevant. The
prayers could be coming from the next room
or halfway around the globe and were just as
effective.

Scientists commenting on the studies were
unanimous in their conclusion that something
was taking place but were at a total loss as to

how to explain it. Some force was at work, but the complete irrelevance of proximity ruled out any known type of energy. The one intriguing clue was postulated by an author who made the analogy to a mysterious quality of quantum particles. Apparently, if these particles were once joined together and then separated, a change induced in one particle would simultaneously cause a change in the now-distant particle—regardless of distance. What this implies, of course, is that in some way we do not understand, everything is connected.

Most of the great religious traditions postulate that either everything was once one and that our current existence is part of a long struggle back to that unity, or that the unity was never destroyed and our sense of separation is in fact an illusion. Within those frameworks, loving-kindness is the prayer that ties us together, that affects us all, regardless of distance.

If this is true, each and every act of kindness done by anyone anywhere resonates out into the world and somehow, mysteriously, invisibly, and perfectly, touches us all.

Kindness
Creates
Happiness and
Peace of Mind

"The more we can love ourselves and attend to all of life around us with a loving, open, connected heart . . . the more we can be in a beautiful place."
—*Brooke Medicine Eagle*

Sometimes life seems terribly unfair. We are given these extraordinarily adept bodies and minds, the ability to speak and reason, the innate knowledge that life can be beautiful and full of joy, and then are left in the dark about how to get there. As we grow up, we are taught all the skills necessary to survive, and precious few of the skills necessary to thrive. Those, for the most part, we must scrap and struggle to attain, usually through the painful process of trial and error.

And yet, in the midst of all this difficult work, we all carry within us a resource of incredible power that can help provide exactly the guidance and encouragement we so desperately need—the human heart. Our hearts do not think, they feel; and each and every emotion is a gift of pure insight and a searchlight waiting to be followed.

When we learn to follow our hearts, we discover an amazing thing: The elusive path to happiness is not only brightly lit, it is calling us, sending a continuous stream of messages in a never-ending feedback loop. And each message is wrapped in the tender kindness of the human spirit. The more we hear the call, the more we respond and the stronger the signal and greater the joy.

Kindness begets kindness. As we resonate more and more strongly to the call of our heart, we find the peace of mind that comes from knowing that we are in the right place. The practices in this section focus on many ways that kindness finds to open our hearts to deeper and deeper joy.

Spread It Around

> "Happiness is like jam. You can't spread even a little without getting some on yourself."
>
> —Anonymous

"I was flying home from a business trip at the end of what had been a long, hard day. I was tired and in no mood to be sociable, so of course I ended up sitting next to an unaccompanied five-year-old girl who was going to visit her grandparents. At first, I tried to ignore her, but when we were pulling back from the gate, she was gripping the armrests so hard I could tell she was really scared. So I tried to talk her through the takeoff, telling her everything was going to be fine, that it was like a really exciting ride at the amusement park.

"Once we got airborne, she calmed down a bit and turned to me with these big eyes and told me she had never been to an amusement park. I started laughing, she started talking, and the next thing I knew we were landing. I had sat there for almost two hours, completely engaged in the kind of rambling, freewheeling conversation you can have only with kids. She insisted on introducing me to her grandparents, who were waiting to pick her up; and as I left the terminal, I felt revived, like all the exhaustion of the day had just lifted off of me."

As this traveler found out, amazing and surprising things can happen when we extend ourselves to others. We think we are doing something because the other person is in need, and it ends up that we ourselves are also renewed and refreshed. That's because when we extend ourselves for another, we tap into an eternal river of ever-present happiness just waiting to be drawn upon.

So remember, even when you are feeling drained and without the slightest resources to reach out to another, the very act of making a connection can bring you back to that river to help wash away your exhaustion, cleanse the dirt and grit of the daily grind, and fill you once again with the wonder of life.

*A*ll That's Needed
Is a Change of Heart

> "The most powerful agent of growth and transformation is something much more basic than any technique: a change of heart."
>
> —John Welwood

We know a man named John whose wife died of cancer in her forties, leaving behind three children. The process of helping her die at home, grieving her loss fully and completely, and helping his kids mourn has permanently cracked his heart wide open. Even now, four years later, John seems to glow with a translucent light that affects everyone he meets. Other folks have their hearts opened from less painful experiences—a week-long retreat, perhaps, or a chance encounter with a person like John.

The beauty and mystery of loving-kindness is that is doesn't require any fancy techniques, any method that needs to be perfected, any set rules. It requires just a change of heart—an attitude change in which you start to behave differently from the way you have in the past. Not because you think you should, not because you are afraid something terrible will happen if you don't, but because you feel like it because your heart is open. A change of heart can happen in any number of ways.

What flows from an open heart flows freely and naturally, a commitment to trying to do all the good you can do to yourself, to your loved ones, to strangers, to Mother Earth. We all have the capacity to be open-hearted, but often our hearts get so covered over with wounds and protective armor that we lose the ability to respond in unobstructed ways.

Take a moment right now to examine the state of your heart. Perhaps you want to ask that you will always know how to locate the switch to your heart so that you can check in with it every now and then. Is it wide open, ready and anxious to embrace the world? Or do you need to do some healing or get some rest in order to feel its marvelous fullness?

Self-fullness, not Selfishness

> "Our first step in mind retraining is to establish peace of mind as our single goal. This means thinking of ourselves first in terms of self-fullness, not selfishness."
> —*John Templeton*

"I was married for twenty years to a very wealthy man. It started out all very romantically, like a dream really, but very quickly I realized that he was really much more interested in his job than in me. My role was to be the attractive and attentive wife and hostess. I should have left then, but I was seduced by the money and the lifestyle. I spent most of my time buying things in a long, agonizing attempt to fill up my life, while every year it became more empty and meaningless.

"When I finally left, it took years for me to crawl out of the hole I had dug for myself, and in the process I discovered that the more simply I lived, the happier I got. I went through a long period of divestiture—giving away all the things I had accumulated—and it was almost as if each article of clothing given away, each piece of furniture moved out, lifted some of the weight off my spirit. One of the most enjoyable ways I accomplished this was to organize auctions and garage sales for local nonprofit organizations, using not only my things, but unwanted items donated by all the rich friends in my previous life. One day after virtually everything was gone, I woke up in my beautiful little home surrounded by morning light and not much else, and I realized that I was finally home, that I was full of happiness for the first time in a very long time."

Selfishness stems from ignorance, from not knowing what we really need to make us happy. Since we don't know, we grab anything and everything we can in hopes that some or all of it will do the trick. When we strip away all the false gods and misguided assumptions and seek instead in the silence of our hearts for our deepest needs, we begin the process of becoming our true selves. And the more we become who we were meant to be, the more we truly are full to overflowing and can offer that abundance to everything around us.

Watch Your Thoughts

"The thought manifests as the word; /
The word manifests as the deed; / The
deed develops into habit; / And habit
hardens into character. / So watch the
thought and its ways with care, / And let
it spring from love / Born out of concern
for all beings."

—*The Buddha*

"Some time ago, I worked with a man who
had convinced himself at a very early age that
the world was all about power and control.
He was very good at what he did, but it was
all very coldly calculated. Watching him operate, I saw him becoming more and more a
caricature of his own most cynical projections.

"I remember one Christmas when a number of people he worked with received selec-
tions of expensive wine from him. It was the
kind of gesture that from anyone else would
have been received with pleasure. Instead,
the office joke for weeks revolved around
what he wanted from us that would have ne-
cessitated such an extravagant present.
Some people theorized that he was trying to
purchase status as a decent human being.

Others were certain that it was meant to put us off guard. I wanted to believe that perhaps it had been a genuine gesture of goodwill, but as much as I wanted to believe it, I still couldn't feel it was true.

"I saw him a few months ago, and all the old feelings resurfaced—the difficulty of working around him, the need to always be on guard. But this time it was overshadowed by a deep sadness over what his own convictions had done to him. He couldn't even give a gift from his heart (if indeed it was) without arousing suspicions!"

We must always be careful about our thoughts, because the things we think, our views and opinions about life, about other people, and about love, will seep out into our own lives until we are living them. When we see the world as a mean and cruel place, for us it *will* become mean and cruel. When we think instead about the happiness and joy that surrounds us, we bring them forth like a gentle shower of fall leaves.

Today, pay attention to the messages you send yourself about the nature of the world. What can you observe about your attitudes?

Scatter Joy to Keep It

> "Happiness comes from spiritual wealth, not material wealth. . . . Happiness comes from giving, not getting. If we try hard to bring happiness to others, we cannot stop it from coming to us also. To get joy, we must give it, and to keep joy, we must scatter it."
>
> —John Templeton

There once lived a man who decided to dedicate his life to helping others. He went about his task in a very quiet way, showing up to help a neighbor repair a roof or harvest a field, then returning home to tend his own small field. He was a good farmer and was thus able to grow many beautiful vegetables, which he gave away to those in need. One day, a terrible storm came and destroyed his home as well as his fields. His neighbors, grateful for all the kindness he had shown them, rebuilt his home twice as big, planted new crops in his fields, and filled his yard with fat pigs and healthy chickens.

Looking over this bounty, the man determined that he had so much, he could expand his efforts to help others to the surrounding villages. Rather than hoard what he had, he spent it freely, constantly looking for ways to make people happy. Soon, his deeds were spoken of far and wide, and his name was praised throughout the land. People began to make pilgrimages to his farm because he was such a peaceful and loving person that just to be in his presence was a blessing. When he died after a long and joy-filled life, his village decided to preserve his home as a shrine so that whoever came there would be reminded of the magnificence of a life lived in service to others.

In our own, unique way, we can have as much impact as this mythical farmer. We don't have to harvest our neighbor's field or give away all that we possess. All it takes is a commitment to scatter joy. Just take a look around and see where it can be sown.

Open to the Wellspring of Happiness

> "When we remember the good things we have done, the times of generosity and caring, the times of holding back from hurting someone, we can rejoice in our own goodness. We do good because it frees the heart. It opens us to a well-spring of happiness."
>
> —*Sharon Salzberg*

"Sometimes I think we would be lost without children to remind us of who we are. Last Saturday, I was working in the kitchen when my two youngsters came running in, absolutely glowing with happiness. My daughter, the youngest at four years old, blurts out, 'Mommy, Mommy, we carried Mrs. Gertz's groceries in for her, she asked us and we did it!' They were so happy about having helped my elderly neighbor, you would have thought someone had just promised them a trip to Disneyland.

"I know that helping others is always rewarding to me, but sometimes I know it just in my head; somehow that wonderful feeling of being your best self gets lost in all daily routine. Standing there, looking at their happy faces, brought it all back so strongly."

Life can get so busy and complicated sometimes that we lose track of what makes us happy. Fortunately, we don't need to leave notes around to remind us; we can let children—our own or those of others—or our own hearts lead the way. They act like powerful magnets, drawing us back, revealing to us that much of what has brought us the greatest happiness is not the latest fashion or a fancy new car, but doing the simplest of acts for someone else.

Give to Get

> "Peace is not something you wish for; it's something you make, something you do, something you are, and something you give away!"
>
> —*Robert Fulghum*

"The other day as I was going into a fast-food restaurant, there was a homeless man standing outside, asking for money. I bought an extra hamburger and went back outside to give it to him before returning to eat my own lunch. I saw out the window that he had started to unwrap the burger and then, noticing something across the street, he stopped, rewrapped the burger, and left. Curious, I walked over to the window and watched as he crossed the street and, with a flourish and a bow, gave the hamburger to a homeless woman with a small child who were sitting on the sidewalk."

If you speak with homeless people, they will often tell you that the folks who generally do the kindest deeds for them are themselves homeless—or close to it. There is something about sharing a difficult experience that sensitizes you to the suffering of others and awakens a desire to alleviate that suffering.

Those of us who are fortunate enough not to have had such difficulties need a different entry way: a conscious decision to act. So many of us want peace of mind but do nothing to create it; want love but do not commit loving acts. Kindness, love, compassion, and all the other affirmative values we desire in our lives don't just happen to us; they are generated by our decision to cultivate them within ourselves and then share them with others. If we nourish them, tend them with care, and freely give of them to others, then and only then will our lives be full of the positive attributes we long for.

What quality of mind do you long for in your life? What action can you take today that will help foster that quality? It doesn't have to be something big—a tiny step will do.

Cherish the Cords
of Kindness

"When kindness has left people, even for
a few moments, we become afraid of
them for their reason has left them."
—Willa Cather

"I witnessed a scene once that really fright-
ened me. It was when I was in high school
and a bunch of friends and I had gone to the
county fair on a Saturday night. Sometime
after midnight when most of who was left at
the fairgrounds was drunken high-school and
college kids, a fight broke out between a
bunch of the guys from the local university
and a gang of 'townees.' It lasted only about
ten minutes before the police broke it up, but
it seemed like forever.

"That was years ago, but it is as clear as if
it happened yesterday, because something
happened to the people, not just those fighting, but much of the 'audience' as well. It was
like this terrifying hand had passed over the
crowd, sucking out all of their decency, leaving a pack of vicious wild animals in its wake."

The language we use when we talk about explosive anger is instructive. We talk about "losing" control of our temper, or we simply say we "lost it." But it is not our *temper* that we lose, it is our humanity; and it is not *control* that we lose, but our connection to the divine. This fall from grace is sometimes obvious, but every time we begin to simmer, snap, and harden toward another, we are in the process of abandoning our humanity. Every act of disrespect, condescension, and judgment severs our connection to one another, for kindness and understanding are the sacred cords that bind us together. In their absence, we drift into the horrible abyss.

Sometimes holding onto that connection, particularly when we are provoked, is very difficult. At times like those, we need to call upon all our resources to quiet our minds and hold onto our reason so that we might extend rather than sever the cords of kindness.

It doesn't have to be something as extreme as a gang fight. Every time we curb our temper toward our spouse, children, or pet, we become agents of human connection rather than participants in its breach.

Secrets of Happiness

> "We learn the inner secret of happiness
> when we learn to direct our inner drives,
> our interest and our attention to some-
> thing outside ourselves."
>
> —*Ethel Percy Andrus*

"Just after college, I dated a man for three
years and almost ended up married to him.
He had many wonderful qualities, but he was
obsessed with success. When we were together, he was getting an MBA, and during
that time he was so busy that he drifted farther and farther away emotionally. Our part-
ing was not exactly elegant, and I didn't see
or hear from him for almost fifteen years until
I got a call last week.

"We got together to talk, and first thing he
said was, 'Boy, was I ever a fool to let you
go.' He had gone directly from school into a
very high-powered corporate environment
and risen quickly. The day he was promoted
to vice-president, he quit. He told me it was
supposedly his dream come true, but instead
of being elated, the news sent him into a tail-
spin of depression. He had spent so much

time getting ahead that he had no love in his life—no wife, no children, no meaningful work. Now he runs a consulting company for environmental nonprofits that are trying to establish recycling programs in their communities, and has recently begun a new relationship."

We all want to be happy. And in the past few decades, it was generally thought that happiness was something we could achieve by concentrating on ourselves—in the seventies, on self-improvement through psychotherapy; in the eighties, on the personal acquisition of as much material wealth as possible. And though those things are not in themselves bad—indeed, they are quite useful—they have not given most of us the happiness we seek.

Now, more and more people are recognizing that an exclusively self-focus does not foster joy, peace of mind, or richness of spirit. Rather, it is by reaching out and connecting with those around us that our hearts are filled. If you have been caught up in "me, me, me" and feel empty as a consequence, the good news is that it is never too late to begin reaching out to others. It's easier than you think.

You Are Not Alone

> "Gentleness is everywhere in daily life, a sign that faith rules through ordinary things: through cooking and small talk, through storytelling, making love, fishing, tending animals and sweet corn and flowers, through sports, music and books, raising kids—all the places where the gravy soaks in and grace shines through. Even in a time of elephantine vanity and greed, one never has to look far to see the campfires of gentle people."
>
> —*Garrison Keillor*

"I was driving home from work one day and saw a small truck about half a mile ahead of me swerve and then suddenly flip over onto the side of the road. My stomach instantly knotted up, and as I approached, I saw with growing disbelief at least forty cars speed past without stopping. I too found myself wanting desperately to keep going, to put distance between myself and that smashed truck. But something inside me would not allow me to flee.

"Nervous and scared at what I might find, I pulled over and ran to the partially opened door. Inside, a young man, bleeding from his head, was trying to climb out. As I leaned in to help him, I saw a woman reaching in from behind me to turn off the engine. Across the cabin, another man was leaning in to help undo the driver's safety belt. Together, we eased the young man out of the car while another woman called an ambulance on her car phone. The four of us stayed and did what we could for the injured man until the ambulance arrived, and as it was driving away, I looked around me and there were almost a dozen anxious faces staring back at me."

Sometimes it's easy to feel that you are the only person out there trying to be kind and considerate, so why should you bother? Garrison Keillor's quote reminds us that we are not alone; that despite what it looks like on television and in the newspaper, despite the evidence to the contrary we seem to see all around us, we are a part of a vast network of well-intentioned people seeking the good and loving well. By believing that, we make it ever more true.

$\mathcal{T}$he Circle of Happiness

> "It is one of the most beautiful compensations of this life that no man can sincerely try to help another without helping himself."
>
> —*Ralph Waldo Emerson*

"I was about four months into starting up my own landscape architecture business when a friend called me in a panic, asking if I could help her out. She had a catering operation that was supposed to put on an important luncheon that weekend, and three of her employees had gotten stranded by a snowstorm. My own schedule was stressed enough, but I agreed to help, even though I had no experience as a waiter.

"During the luncheon, to my mortification, I spilled half a plate of rice pilaf onto a man's lap. He was very gracious and made some comment about me being new to this kind of thing. Very embarrassed, I confessed that I was actually a landscape architect, more comfortable slinging bags of fertilizer than balancing gourmet delicacies.

"Two days later he called me, having

tracked me down through the catering company, and asked me to bid on a job landscaping the front of his office. I ended up doing the work, and when the job was finished, I went by to pick up my payment. I saw that he had erected in his front yard a small sign saying "Landscaped by Ross Gardens" with my name and phone number on it. The place was such a showpiece that it launched my career. Five years later, I am still getting business from that little sign."

Isn't it amazing how life works? You never know where *anything* will lead! You take your cousin's daughter to a matinee as a favor and bump into the man you end up marrying. You agree to organize the charity ball for the hospital and meet the heart surgeon who eventually saves your mother's life.

When we extend ourselves to others, we reap not only the peace of mind and satisfaction of having done the right thing, but we place ourselves where we should be—in the flow of our lives, fully open to the next mysterious and surprising turn of fate. For the next few days, try saying yes to everything that is not actually harmful and see where it leads you.

Uncap Your Spirit

> "All of us need to be touched in the deepest parts of our lives, to have our spirit uncapped. If you uncap it, it will go everywhere. That's why we're here."
> —*The Reverend Cecil Williams*

"As we are growing up, most of us wonder what our purpose is supposed to be. I know I did a lot, and it was really frustrating because for the longest time it seemed like it was right there—just over my shoulder—but every time I would turn to look, it would vanish. Then a few years ago, I got laid off and for the first time in years suddenly had all this time on my hands. I decided to hike back into the mountains for a few days just to unwind, and found myself sitting in the midst of a beautiful valley with tears streaming down my face. It felt like my whole life up to that point was leading me to this moment. The simple power and beauty of all that nature just poured through me, washing away everything and leaving this incredible sense of peacefulness and joy.

"Since then, my purpose has moved from

behind my shoulder right into the center of my heart. I realized that it was my destiny to lead wilderness trips, particularly for teenagers who have never been out in nature. Now, every time I bring another unsuspecting group of kids into the midst of Mother Nature, I can see on their faces that the magic is working on them too."

Each of us, in our precious uniqueness, is an instrument of the divine. Our task on this earth is to discover the purpose for which we have been sent here. The answer is always there, hovering beside us, waiting for the moment when we are touched in the deepest part of our souls.

If you have discovered your life's purpose, take a moment to give thanks. If you are still searching, know that life is working on you and with you, and ask that soon you will have your spirit uncapped so that it may flow out into the world and do its holy work.

Spread Mental Sunshine

> "Mental sunshine will cause the flowers of peace, happiness, and prosperity to grow upon the face of the earth. Be a creator of mental sunshine."
>
> —*Anonymous graffiti*

"I worked for an insurance company for five years while I was going to school at night. It was a very difficult and stressful time of my life, made infinitely worse by the committed pettiness of the company. We lived by production quotas and the time clock; we even had to clock out and in for our breaks. The whole office of about forty people was just beaten down by the cruel regimen, except for one woman who I swear brought us all through each day.

"She was the most cheerful person I ever met. Fortunately for us, her job was to drop off and pick up the files we were supposed to be churning out, so she passed by all of our desks several times a day. No matter what, she walked through that office like a radiant beam of sunshine on a heavily overcast day. I don't know how she came by such a joyful disposition, but I, for one, never would have made it without her."

The attitude we have toward the world affects everyone around us. When we are down or anxious, we act like miniature black holes, drawing off the surrounding energy and joyfulness. When we are able to move through our lives radiating happiness, we are like mobile suns, bathing everyone in the warmth of our rays.

This doesn't mean we should fake it— there's no turn-off like phony cheer. Rather, whenever you truly feel like it, give the gift of your radiance to those around you so that they all might be bathed by warmth and good cheer.

𝒯he Delight of Random Kindness

> "Kindness is always undeserved. And
> what rejoices man's heart / is precisely
> what he is given as a sheer gift . . . a gift
> which / he has not deserved."
>
> —*Rudolf Bultmann*

"When I was younger, I dated this woman for about six months, and really acted like a jerk. I wasn't in love with her, but I had nothing else going on so I just kept seeing her. The longer it went on, the worse I acted. It was almost as if even though I didn't have the courtesy to tell her she didn't mean anything to me, I was unconsciously trying to show her by treating her like dirt.

"One night after I had dropped by to sleep with her and left immediately afterward, I ended up running out of gas out in the middle of nowhere. As I sat there hoping someone would come by, I kept thinking that I had been acting so badly that I really deserved to be stranded. I waited for almost half an hour, and then an old Rambler went by, slowed down, and backed up. Inside was a little gray-haired old lady, which really surprised me since we were way off the main road, it was nearing midnight, and she didn't know me from Adam. She drove me fifteen miles to an all-night gas station and then back again—it was probably one o'clock in the morning by the time she was on her way again.

"She'll never know it, but that old lady in the Rambler spurred a turning point in my life. I figured that if she could treat someone she never met before so kindly, I could at least not mistreat someone I knew well."

Kindness is a wonderful paradox. It is not something we can earn: We can't put in our time at the local charity, try to be nice, and then *expect* kindness. It simply comes when and where it does. At the same time, it *is* something we all deserve simply because we are a part of the miracle of creation. So share your kindness randomly, aware that you may never really know the effect your action will have, and treasure each precious offering you receive.

Pluck a Thistle, Plant a Flower

> "All my life I have tried to pluck a thistle and plant a flower wherever the flower would grow in thought and mind."
>
> —*Abraham Lincoln, inspired by his gentle, beloved mother whose personal credo was kindness to neighbors and strangers*

"Every family has its odd relationships. In my family, it was between my younger brother and my oldest aunt. She suffered from a deforming birth defect and had grown more and more bitter about it as she got older. All of us kids gave her a wide berth except my baby brother, who ignored all her sharp edges and showered her with love and attention.

"It was really something to see. He truly liked her. She would move through a family gathering, pushing people away and muttering under her breath, and he would zoom in and attach himself to her arm and babble on and on about whatever was exciting him at the moment as if she were the best and most attentive audience in the world. As much trouble as we all had understanding their strange bond, there was something very beautiful, almost holy about it. Of course I didn't see that then; I just thought he was a weird kid. But as I grew up, just remembering that odd couple has helped me to look beyond the surface, to try to find and cherish the good inside everyone I come across."

Our world is a shifting ecology of spectacular beauty and prickly thistles, and the balance of thorns to roses is ours to determine. When we come across a tangle of thorns, we can choose to either turn away or help clear a place for roses to blossom. In the end, it is the choices we make, the compassion and kindness we extend, that will decide how thorny or beautiful the world we inhabit will be.

Today, ask yourself to notice where you can pluck a thistle and plant a rose.

Rejoice in Other People's Happiness

> "The quiet, probably unnoticed, sharing in a neighbor's joy, no less than in his sorrow, constitutes an act of kindness."
> —Morris Adler

"Our church sponsors a scholarship that is given each year to the graduating senior with the highest grade-point average. Throughout high school, my best friend, Jody, and I would trade off leading our class. When the final grades were in, I had won by a fraction of a percent. I was very happy, because the scholarship meant being able to go to college, but I felt bad about Jody, because she needed it just as much as I did. I had been notified by mail and of course I wanted to tell Jody, but was also uncertain about how to do it.

"Finally, I got up my courage and drove over to her house. She responded with such unrestrained enthusiasm that I said, 'But I thought *you* wanted to win.' I'll never forget what she replied: 'Of course I did, but I didn't get it and you did, and I'm so happy for you. I'll find a way to go somehow.' I couldn't help it, I just started crying right there on the spot. I was afraid of hurting her, but her reaction made me realize how strong our friendship was."

One of the qualities that Buddhists seek to cultivate is called *mudita*, which is sympathetic joy, the true rejoicing in the prosperity and good fortune of others. This quality challenges some of our deepest assumptions—namely that happiness or success are finite qualities and if someone else possesses them, we will somehow get less.

Sympathetic joy recognizes the interconnection between us—that our neighbor's happiness is truly in some sense our own. Indeed, happiness actually grows as we share it, because, as Buddhist teacher Sharon Salzberg says, "The act of sharing puts us in touch with its source, which is limitless." In this way, sharing in the happiness of others is actually an act of kindness to ourselves, we affirm our belief in the limitlessness of happiness. How do you respond to the happiness of others? Are you joyful or do you feel jealous? Take some time to look at your capacity for sympathetic joy.

The Tao of Kindness

"Mental goodwill is reciprocal. The good thoughts you send out to others will return to you multiplied."
—*Grenville Kleiser*

"I have always believed that when we are presented an opportunity to show kindness to someone, the world is giving us a gift that is its own reward. So when I found myself on a long intercontinental flight, sitting next to a young woman with two small, restless children, I dove right in. We had a great time and eventually the kids fell asleep.

"As the young woman and I sat talking, I suddenly began feeling light-headed and then increasingly uncomfortable. At one point, she reached over and touched my forehead and said, 'You are burning up.' Through the rest of the trip, she took care of me, cooling me down with a damp washcloth, helping me back and forth to the bathroom—that must have been a sight with our four legs poking out of that tiny compartment—and keeping my spirits up with her genuine concern. It was the worst and the best flight I have ever taken."

There is no mystery to the eternal circle of kindness. When we extend ourselves to another, we are opening our hearts to the world, and with our hearts wide open, we are poised to receive what goodness is there for us. So when you find yourself closing down or drifting away, reconnect to the healing flow of kindness by extending yourself to others. It will come back a hundredfold.

Kindness Generates Love and Compassion

"Compassion—literally 'suffering with'—is born out of feeling the rawness of the heart, which also makes us more sensitive to others."

—John Welwood

The most difficult part of emerging into the world as an effective and blessed participant in the miracle of creation is breaking out of our individual shells. Like tiny hatchlings, we must strain and batter at the shells that surround and isolate us. It can be hard work, and all too often we succumb to the temptation to retreat back into ourselves, where we at least feel safe. But as we emerge and reach out to those closest to us, we hopefully are nourished by their compassion and generosity, and gradually learn how to exercise our own patience, understanding, and ability to give.

Comforted by the warm glow of connection to our loved ones, we are at times tempted to stop there; for the next step, casting out our caring in wider and wider circles, seems fraught with risk of rejection. But as we increase the power and scope of our hearts, we find that we no longer have to force ourselves to be empathetic toward the suffering souls we come across; it simply flows, growing in size until it is like a great river of love and concern. Riding the currents of that river, we are continuously replenished until the task of compassion and understanding becomes our greatest joy.

The practices in this section focus on the expansive nature of this transformation and help us to see that kindness is not simply an act, but a way of being.

$\mathcal{I}$t's for Ourselves

"I love the story about A. J. Muste, who, during the Vietnam War, stood in front of the White House night after night with a candle—sometimes alone. A reporter interviewed him one evening as he stood there in the rain. 'Mr. Muste,' the reporter said, 'do you really think you are going to change the policies of this country by standing out here alone at night with a candle?' A. J. responded, 'Oh, I don't do this to change the country. I do this so the country doesn't change me.'"
—*Andrea Ayvazian*

Recently, we were having dinner with a new acquaintance. She asked us what we do. As a kind of shorthand explanation, we replied, "We're the publishers of *Random Acts of Kindness*. She shrugged and said, "Oh, *that*. Where I come from (the inner city of Detroit), life is too tough to relate to *that*." We immediately thought of A. J. Muste, the sort of person who says: No matter the circumstances, no matter the effect, I do this because it is good for *me* to act this way, to be this type of person.

Practicing kindness is first and foremost for ourselves. It is for keeping our souls supple and our hearts wide open so that, rich or poor, wherever we find ourselves, we stay tender, compassionate, and sensitive.

If our lives are tough, why should we add more pain to them by our attitudes? We can choose how we respond to the difficulties of life. We can either see them as a measure of how rotten the world is, or allow the very challenges we encounter to remind us to have compassion for ourselves and those we meet on our path, for they too are struggling.

It's so easy to allow adversity to harden our hearts. Take a minute right now to look into your heart. Is there is a way you can soften to your own pain, holding it as tenderly as you would a crying baby?

$\mathcal{K}$indness Transcends All Limitations

> "Kindness is a language which the dumb can speak, the deaf can understand."
> —C. N. Bovee

Recently, I spent a year and a half traveling around the world on a tiny budget. When I returned, many of my friends expressed amazement that I could have done it, saying, 'How could you get by in all those countries when you didn't have money or know the languages?'

"Every time I was asked that question, my mind would flood with hundred of memories of all the people I met who had so enthusiastically helped me each and every time I needed assistance. The little Japanese woman who lead me eight blocks out of her way to the address I never could have found by myself; the Indian family that shared their sack of fresh fruit with me on the ship from Mombassa to Bombay; the old Thai woman who brought me buckets of ice and the most delicious soups as I sweated through a three-day fever in her small hotel; the African man who guided me up Mount Kilimanjaro and back in one day; the hundreds of people I met on trains, buses, and street corners who shared their smiles and greetings.

"What was most true was how easy it was. The lack of ability to communicate verbally was no obstacle. Somehow we always made ourselves understood."

Kindness is the universal language. It is the way we express our understanding that we are all simply fellow travelers in this world. Kindness breaks down all walls and crosses all borders. Kindness requires no words, no explanation. It is understood by all and can be practiced by all. In this way, it truly ties us together.

All It Takes Is You

"Blessed is the influence of one true, loving, human soul on another."
—*George* Eliot

"I don't want to tell the story of my childhood. I've done it enough already, I know how painful it was, and now all I want to do is keep working to put the pieces of my life together.

"But there is one part of the story I will always want to talk about: the day I met Claire. When I met her, I was at the very bottom and looked it—without home, without hope, and without the energy to care anymore. Her job was to scour the streets for the castoffs of society and try to help them. She found me and took me under her wing, getting me food and temporary shelter but, more important, treating me with respect even though I was the last person to think I deserved it.

"She never lectured me and never preached to me; she was just always warm and friendly and encouraging. She treated me like I was a human being, and, to my own surprise, I started to believe it was true. No one had ever been so nice to me. For me, that was the real beginning of my life. This year, on the anniversary of the day she dragged me off the streets, I went back down to the shelter she works at, with balloons and a huge birthday cake and threw myself a party."

Power is not something we often associate with kindness, but in truth kindness is the source of the greatest and most lasting power—the power to change lives. And unlike all other forms of power, kindness can do no harm, only good.

We often don't recognize the true power of kindness because it is so simple. How could it be that the smallest acts make such a dramatic difference? But they do. So become a catalyst for transformation and unleash your power into the world.

You Don't Have to Think Your Way Through

> "Go to the truth beyond the mind. Love is the bridge."
>
> —*Stephen Levine*

We all have been so bombarded with horror stories about Bosnia recently that it appears like hell on earth. But what we don't often hear are the incredible stories of simple humanity at work. For even in the midst of devastation and destruction, compassion does flower. A friend of ours just returned after working with the Red Cross and told the following story.

He was stuck in a small village near a ravine with soldiers on both ridges shooting back and forth. During a lull in the fighting, a young woman ran out of a small house in the ravine to try to drag her goat back to safety. Just as she reached the goat, the shooting resumed and she was hit. Instantly, all fighting stopped, and one of the attacking soldiers jumped up and ran down the ravine toward her. In the eerie silence that followed, the soldier examined her and began calling for a medic. Two soldiers from the defending troops ran down with a gurney and together they carried her back to the village while the first soldier returned to his line. The fighting never resumed, and by the next day the attacking soldiers were gone.

When we act from the place that is beyond our intellect or rationale, we access love to get there. In some ways, it makes no sense to pull someone from a burning car, to give a meal to a homeless man, or take a gift to a dying child. After all, you can be killed, the homeless man will no doubt be hungry again tomorrow, and the child is still going to die. But when, in love, we go to the truth beyond the mind, we know that everything we do matters. And we can't *not* act.

Today, don't worry about thinking about being loving. Just follow your heart.

Bless Us into Usefulness

> "In the words of one great prayer: 'Bless me into usefulness.'"
>
> —*Sogyal Rinpoche*

"A story I want to tell was passed down in my family from my great-grandfather. He was a young captain from Pennsylvania fighting in the Civil War. In preparation for a coming battle, he had requisitioned a beautiful Georgia plantation home as a field hospital. He told the lady of the house to leave before the battle started, but she responded, 'I am staying. There will be wounded and I can be useful.' For four days, her land was occupied by her enemy and was turned into a bloody battlefield while she tirelessly did everything she could to ease the suffering of the wounded and the dying Union soldiers. Word of her care spread through the troops, and when they were leaving, every man turned and saluted as they passed her home.

"My great-grandfather said that it was the most enduring memory he had of that horrible war, because it reminded him that even in the midst of an incredibly brutal and savage experience, one person's simple kindness could still shine through."

One of the few things about life that is certain is that it never turns out as you plan. You may set out to be a writer, for example, but then life gets into the act and you must care for your dying mother or your newborn child, and suddenly you find yourself launched in an entirely different direction. That's why, like the Confederate woman, it's best to try to have a flexible attitude toward what does happen and, wherever you find yourself, ask: "How can I be of use here?"

One very simple and effective way to do this is to take a reflective moment each morning to ask that you be of use that day, that all your talents, skills, and influence be utilized for the greatest good.

Keep Compassion in the Foreground

> "My mission is to express my feeling about the importance of kindness, compassion, and the true sense of brotherhood . . . If I practiced anger or jealousy or bitterness, no doubt my smile would disappear."
>
> —The Dalai Lama, explaining why he smiles even in the face of the destruction of Tibet by the Chinese

As the Dalai Lama demonstrates, hate begets hate, and love begets love. If we want to change the world for the better, we cannot respond with violence, anger, or cruelty—even to those who may be mistreating us. That will ensure only that the cycle of misery continues.

This is not to say that we don't have a right to protect ourselves—the Dalai Lama, for example, left Tibet so that he wouldn't be imprisoned or killed. But it does mean that we must be scrupulously careful not to contribute our measure to the hate that is already abundant in the world, by instead practicing love and compassion—even toward those who may have wounded us.

We each have at least one person we've thrown out of our hearts for bad behavior—the parent we're holding a grudge against, the ex-spouse we rail about, the sibling we "can't stand." Can you make room in your heart today for this person so that you will add to the compassion in the world and diminish the hate by at least one person?

Keep the Faith

> "I believe that man will not merely en-
> dure; he will prevail. He is immortal, not
> because he alone among the creatures
> has an inexhaustible voice, but because
> he has a soul, a spirit capable of kind-
> ness and compassion."
> —William Faulkner

"I was raised by parents who really believed
that life was about service. I think that's why,
when I became an adult, that doing what I
could, believing in the good, and continuing
even when I was discouraged came naturally
to me. But for some reason recently, the constant battering of bad news and a series of
personal setbacks finally pushed me into a
state of despair. As much as I wanted to believe that things would improve, as much as I
desperately wanted to believe that in time we
can turn our troubled world into a joyful para-
dise, I was on the verge of giving up.

"Then one day when I was getting out of
my car, I saw a little boy leaning over a bird
in the next-door neighbor's yard. The bird had
flown into a plate-glass window and injured

itself, and the boy was building a small nest in a shoe box to take the bird home and care for it. Seeing him tenderly lift that bird was like the ringing of a bell. I realized that caring is a part of all of us. Like that small boy, we all move through life with the capacity and desire to love buried in our hearts. We may lose track, get too busy and too distracted to pay attention, get bogged down in the day-to-day troubles of life, but it is always there, ready to be awakened."

What makes us humans different from all other life, as far as we know, is our capacity to be empathetic—and to be aware of that ability. Indeed, our defining quality as human beings is that we can care. In moments of despair, when all else fails, we can remember that, and have faith in our collective ability for compassion.

*A*ll Beings Want to Be Happy

> "Every human being is your counterpart. Every other human being possesses and embodies aspects of yourself: your dreams, your sorrows, your hope that your life will not be like a dirty joke."
> —*Daphne Rose Kingma*

"I'm eighty years old and stuck in the hospital with a broken hip. That's the thing that usually kills off us old ladies, so everyone is tiptoeing around me, but I'm not ready to go—even though this crabby nurse of mine has made me think twice about it a few times.

"The other day, my granddaughter brought in a tape of Mozart's sonatas, and it was playing when young Miss Nurse Sourpuss came in with my midday medication. I thought for sure she was going to tell me to turn off the music, but instead she started humming along and smiling to beat the band. I asked her if she liked Mozart, and she sat there for ten minutes, telling me about how she had played the piano since she was five and was working extra shifts to save up so she could go to music school. There I was, thinking she was more of a pain than my aching hip, and inside she had a song in her heart."

Compassion is the art of recognizing that, at the core, there is really no difference between us, that we each have sorrows and joys, pain and pleasures, and that we are all muddling through life as best we can. However, it's not always easy to remember, especially when someone is driving us crazy.

That's why the Buddhists have a practice to remind themselves of this fundamental connection. Called "the loving-kindness meditation," it has many variations, but one includes the recitation of the sentence: "Just as I want to be happy, so do all beings want to be happy." Saying it over and over reminds one that at the most profound level, we truly are the same—all desiring freedom from suffering. To actively remember this is to touch that connection between us all and to be able to act more often from compassion rather than condemnation.

Why not give it a try for a few days and see what happens?

Believe in the Power
of Loving-Kindness

"The secret of improved plant breeding, apart from scientific knowledge, is love. While I was conducting experiments to make spineless cacti, I often talked to the plants. . . . 'You have nothing to fear,' I would tell them. 'You don't need your defensive thorns. I will protect you.' Gradually the useful plant of the desert emerged in a thornless variety."
—*Botanist Luther Burbank*

We were doing a radio interview in Portland, Oregon, about *Random Acts of Kindness*, and an obviously very old man called to tell a story of a couple who had taken him in for a few months when he was a young man. It was a simple story told in a very shaky voice, and afterward we asked him if he would mind telling us how long ago it had happened. He replied, "Seventy-five years ago, and a day doesn't go by that I don't remember those people."

Of all the thousands of stories of kindness we've heard, that one always sticks with us

214

because it illustrates so simply and beautifully the awesome power of kindness. Two people's compassion and hospitality offered to a young man seventy-five years ago is still echoing strongly in the world—throughout the life of the man they helped, over the airwaves of Portland, and now here on these pages for you to share.

It is so seemingly implausible and yet so undeniably true that the simplest acts of loving-kindness are the most powerful force in our world. So powerful is the force of love that it is the foundation of all religions and the unbreakable thread that binds us together as a tribe, a community, a nation, and a world. By believing in the depth and lasting strength of kindness, we can remember to employ it as often as we can.

Today, think of one nice thing you have done for someone and picture the effect it might have had on the person you assisted. Think of the old man in this story and imagine how the world might have changed from your one tiny act.

Compassion, not Codependence

> "Mature love and healthy compassion
> are not dependent, but interdependent,
> born out of a deep respect for ourselves
> as well as others."
>
> —*Jack Kornfield*

"My husband and I had been together for only a couple of years and were trying to juggle new careers and part-time parenting of his two kids, when a friend became extremely sick. Sheila had no family and no other friends around, so it seemed like we were the only ones who could help her. After she got out of the hospital, we moved her into our house, where she stayed for nine months. From the outside, it must have looked like a very generous act, but in reality it was an almost constant cycle of tension, anxiety, anger, and guilt. I didn't want her there. I was resentful about caring for the kids as well as her, and yet at the same time I would feel incredibly guilty for being upset.

"As time went on, I began to see that I was

doing it because I thought I *had* to. I had been raised to sacrifice my needs for those of my mother, who had a chronic illness, and so when the situation with Sheila came up, it fit exactly into my old pattern."

In this culture, our capacity for true compassion is often limited by an incomplete development of a healthy sense of self. Because of our early wounds, our giving may be based in fear—something bad will happen to me if I don't do what you want—and we may end up losing ourselves through codependent support of someone else.

So how can we tell healthy compassion from codependence? Codependence arises, writes Jack Kornfield, "when we have forgotten our *own* role in the balancing act of human relationships . . . so intent on caring for others or on pleasing or pacifying them or avoiding conflict with them that we don't clearly face our own needs, our own situation."

One of the ways to avoid falling into the trap of false compassion is to inquire into your reasons for doing something and to make sure you put yourself into the picture.

Express Your Greatness

"Everyone can be great because everyone can serve."

—Martin Luther King Jr.

"I live in a low-income apartment complex. A lot of my neighbors are single mothers struggling to get by, and sometimes you can almost feel despair all around you. It is just so difficult to raise kids, work, and try to make something better of your life at the same time.

"But there is this one man who lives there who I swear must have been given to us by some higher power. He is both physically and mentally handicapped but has managed to take care of himself by working part-time at a fast-food place and collecting cans and bottles to recycle. He knows us all by name and greets us all when we leave each morning and return each evening. He's always there to help out, although we are all really careful not to take advantage of him. He loves kids, and there isn't a day when at least one of the kids from the complex can't be spotted hanging around the playground with him, being pushed on the swing or playing in the sandbox. When you need to rush out to the store, he is always willing to keep an eye on the kids for a while. But mostly, he is just always there, always smiling, reminding us that we are more than all our problems."

Greatness comes in all shapes and sizes, and most true heroes are unsung. You don't have to be a Martin Luther King Jr. to serve the world. Each of us has our own particular talent or ability, and when we offer it to the world around us, we are expressing our unique greatness. What is your magnificent and singular gift that the world is waiting to receive?

Do It When You Least Feel Like It

> "When your bow is broken and your last arrow spent, then shoot, shoot with your whole heart."
>
> —*Zen saying*

"I had friends visiting from out of town, and as usual we had packed four days of visiting into two. One of them wanted to get together with a friend of his. I was overtired and just wanted to relax, but I finally relented. We ended up driving all over to pick him up, and when we were first introduced, it was obvious to me that he was suffering in some way.

"At one point, we ended up sitting alone together. There I was, exhausted and sitting across from a man who for all appearances was ready to drain whatever meager reserves I had left. I didn't want to reach out to him, but I did, and the result was really startling. We talked for only about ten minutes, but it completely changed him. I think he just needed someone to listen from their heart. The most amazing thing is that it completely reenergized *me*. Ten minutes of real, intense human contact and I felt better than I had all day."

It seems like such a paradox. When we come to the very edge, when we are certain that we cannot do what we feel we should do, that is when we are most open to being transformed by the doing. We may complain that we have no reserves, but precisely because we feel we have nothing left to give, our minds can no longer get in the way—and that is when magic can happen. When we extend ourselves despite our fatigue, our concern for the other person connects us to the great wellspring of love, and we ourselves are washed in it.

Of course, it is not healthy to run on chronic overload, and sometimes the best thing you can do for yourself and everyone else is to take a nap. But if you occasionally find yourself feeling tired and not particularly sociable, try extending yourself anyway and notice how it makes you feel.

Make Kindness
a Calling

"To the good I am good; / to the non-good I am also good, / for Life is goodness. / To the faithful I am faithful; / to the unfaithful I am also faithful, / for Life is faithfulness . . . / the person of calling accepts them all / as his or her children."
—*Tao Te Ching*

"I was in the seminary for three years. It was a wonderful and troubled time in my life. I wanted so desperately to devote my life to God, but I felt out of place and anxious the whole time I was there. I could not understand it—I was surrounded by wonderful people, I was doing exactly what I had always wanted to do, and yet I grew more and more unhappy every day.

"Finally, an old priest who was temporarily living with us at the seminary took me under his wing and very gently helped me to untangle the knots of confusion I had wound. It soon became obvious that this was not the life for me. When I protested that I had felt the calling, he told me that all of us will hear

222

the call if we listen carefully—it is the sound of our hearts calling us to love one another, and each of us must find our own way of responding."

If we listen to our hearts, we too can hear them calling, calling for us to treat each other with love and respect, to act with generosity and compassion. Each of us has his or her own path of service. Dedicate yourself to the call of your heart and see where it leads you.

Don't Fake It

> "Authentic kindness (as opposed to play-acting 'nice' because we are motivated by fear or guilt), a from-the-heart desire to reach out in love and compassion, is a reflection of who we really are—beings of love."
>
> —*Sue Patton Thoele*

"I have lived in a retirement home for five years. I'm old, can barely get around anymore, but I still have most of my faculties about me. Every Christmas, the ladies from a local service group show up to 'brighten' our holiday. Trouble is, for most of them it just doesn't go off too well. They are all smiles and pleasantness, but it's all a performance. I think seeing so many elderly people scares the daylights out of them—and that just stretches their smiles even more.

"But last year, I got a real treat. One of the ladies had dragged along her son, and while they were all fussing around, he came up to me and said, 'How'd you ever get so old?' His mom was embarrassed as could be, but I just bust out laughing. I told him I didn't know how it happened, I just kept living. Then I told his mom to leave him with me for a while to keep me company. I had more fun talking to that boy than I've had in years. He was just a pure honest kid who was willing to really talk to a wrinkled-up old man."

Kindness is bred in authenticity—our being our true selves. It cannot be put on because by its very nature it is the genuine caring for another.

So just be yourself, not what you think you should be, not what anyone else expects you to be. The better you get at being yourself, the more you will naturally embody loving-kindness.

$\mathcal{T}$he Levels of Generosity

> "For most of us, generosity is a quality that must be developed. We have to respect that it will grow gradually; otherwise our spirituality can become idealistic and imitative, acting out the image of generosity before it has become genuine."
>
> —Jack Kornfield

"My grandmother was always a generous woman, but as she got older, her giving accelerated to the point that when I came to visit her one day, some men were hauling her dining-room set out the door. I was upset because I didn't want to see her with nothing left. She sat me down and said, 'Sweetheart, the key thing is timing. I have no desire to live in poverty, but I would love to time it so that the day I died I had nothing left.'

Buddhists believe that generosity consists of three levels that we progress along as we practice. The first is *tentative giving*, in which we're not sure we want to do it. For example, we have an old sofa we're thinking of giving to Goodwill but we hesitate: What if someday we need it? Finally, we decide it's okay to give away and discover happiness and freedom in the giving of it, what the Buddhists call "the first joys of giving."

This makes it easier to give from the second level, which is *sisterly or brotherly giving*, an equal sharing of both energy and material goods as if to a loved one. With this type of giving, we feel no hesitation, rather a sense of "I have this, so let us all share in it." Friendship, openness, and a spirit of joy prevail.

The most developed generosity is called *royal giving*, in which we take such delight in the welfare and happiness of others that we give the best of what we have, rather than just an equal part. With this kind of giving, writes Jack Kornfield, "it is as if we become a natural channel for the happiness of all around us."

We can't vault to the higher levels of giving by the force of our will. Rather, as we practice tentative giving and compassion toward ourselves, the happiness and satisfaction we feel will naturally encourage us to the other levels. The most important thing is to be genuine.

Come from the Heart

> "The mind cannot long act the role of the heart."
>
> —François la Rochefoucauld

In order to bring more love into our lives, we need to learn to live from our hearts rather than our heads. Our hearts, not our minds, are the initiators of all genuine behavior. If we try to act like we "think" we should, we are doubly handicapped. First, more often than not we are responding to some external rules of behavior which may or may not be appropriate for us at any given moment.

Second, we end up creating our own internal conflicts because our wonderful minds, as incredible as they are, cannot control how we feel. If we say to ourselves, for example, I *must remember to be nice to my coworkers*, it becomes a task that we "should" do, something else for our busy minds to remember. But if we cultivate a stance of open-heartedness toward ourselves and those around us, we will not *have* to remember—it will be our inclination rather than duty.

228

Becoming open-hearted is less a process of trying and more one of softening, first toward ourselves, then toward the people around us and the circumstances of life itself. As we develop compassion for our own fears and foibles, cradling them as we would a tiny infant, we can also more often look with softened eyes at those around us and respond from the fullness of our hearts.

Take a moment now to look kindly upon yourself. What hardships have you been going through? What unmet needs do you have that are causing you pain? In this moment, can you offer yourself a bit of solace and comfort? You deserve your own mercy and compassion; after all, you are doing the best you can.

The Work of Loving-Kindness

> "This is the work and the power of loving-kindness, the embrace that allows no separation between self, others, and events—the affirmation and honoring of a core goodness in others and oneself."
> —*Sharon Salzberg*

"When I got divorced, my world fell apart. Being married had been my life. I did everything I could to make it work, and when it fell apart and my ex-husband blamed me for everything, I felt as if everything I had done had been reduced to nothing.

"For a couple of years, I was caught in a confused swirl of bitter recriminations and blame until one day when I was talking to friend and she chimed in about what an evil jerk my ex-husband was. The minute she said it, I knew she was wrong. He had certainly acted badly—but then so had I. The truth was, I know him very well. I know about his sweetness and good humor and his generosity. I also know all about his demons, the issues that he is struggling with so unsuccessfully, the way he tries and fails and tries again. To my surprise and delight, I realized that I still cared for him and really hoped he would find his way."

We have all had the experience of forgiving someone we love—our parents, our children, our lovers, our friends—of looking past their hurtful behavior and seeing them for the flawed but good people they truly are. If we can do it once, we can do it anywhere and anytime. For one of the greatest challenges in life is to be able to cast the net of under-standing and compassion in broader and broader sweeps.

Can we really see the good in ourselves and those around us? Can we truly cultivate a continuing sense of the deep connection between ourselves, others, and events such that a wound to one is a injury to us all? This is the challenge of loving-kindness, to be able to live our lives in deep connection to all around us in this profound way.

Will We Be Able to Answer?

> "At the end of life, our questions are very simple: Did I live fully? Did I love well?"
> —Jack Kornfield

The shallow and cynical side of human nature is painful to observe. A while back, you could spot people walking around with T-shirts that said, "The one who dies with the most toys wins." If serious, it was terrifying; hopefully, however, people wore it as a humorous response to the feeding frenzy of accumulation that seems to be so virulent in our society.

Rampant consumerism and "me, me, me-ism" makes us want to somehow wake everyone up by screaming, "Time is passing, your life is slipping away, forget the toys and get on with living!" One of the best articulations of this wake-up call is this inspiring poem from Conari author Dawna Markova. May it enliven you today.

I will not die an unlived life.
I will not live in fear
of falling or catching fire.
I choose to inhabit my days,
to allow my living to open me,
to wake me less afraid, more accessible,
to loosen my heart
until it becomes a wing,
a touch, a promise.
I choose to risk my significance,
to live
so that which comes to me as seed
goes to the next as blossom
and that which comes to me as blossom
goes on as fruit.

Kindness Feeds the Body and Soul

"A word of kindness is better than a fat pie."

—*Russian proverb*

$\mathcal{I}$n many religious traditions, the circle is the symbol of the divine. Certainly in the complex process of human life, the circle is a powerful, transforming metaphor. The issues we struggle with as individuals return to us time and again, altered by the last circuit around, with ever-increasing urgency until we master the lessons they carry, and then with ever-increasing subtlety and wisdom.

So too with the overall process of our lives. We begin tiny, helpless, and needy. One of our very first words, both precious and oddly embarrassing to our parents, is "mine." We grab and demand, stake out and defend, declare and insist. As unartful as it is, it is a necessary part of building our own individual foundation. And from that foundation, we learn to expand ourselves outward—to offer consolation, to provide compassion and understanding, to give and receive love, to expand our hearts in ever-broadening circles.

Until in the end, we have built such a powerful and pulsating web of connections that we look around and see that it is all "ours." All of it—the world of pain, hurt, and suffering, as well as that of extraordinary love, beauty, peace, and joy. We are suspended in the nourishing circle of life, tied by unbreakable cords of love to everyone and everything, full participants in the unfolding miracle of life. In this final section, the practices focus on the broadest and deepest spiritual aspects of kindness.

The Benefits
of Doing Good

"Happiness is not a goal; it is a by-product."
—*Eleanor Roosevelt*

We think we can find happiness by searching for it directly; perhaps a cruise around the world or winning the state lottery will do the trick. As it turns out, the outward expression of our deepest selves is what gives us true happiness—and keeps us healthy as well.

There's a famous study in which elderly people in a nursing home were each given a plant. Half the group were told that they must care for the plant—pay close attention to what the plant needs—food, water, sunshine—and respond to those needs. The other half were told that the plant was theirs to enjoy, but the nursing-home staff would take care of it.

After a year, researchers compared the two groups and found that those who had cared for their plants were much more physically and emotionally healthy than the group who hadn't been responsible for their plants' welfare. Similar studies show that caring for a pet strengthens the immune system.

If the simple act of caring for a flower or a kitten can produce both health and happiness, there must be something essential in our mind/body system that craves the chance to nurture and support growth of all kind. Put more simply, our very organism *needs to love to stay alive*—and that love can be expressed in myriad ways that take virtually no time or energy.

What ways does your body and soul long to express love right now? What can you do, in this moment, no matter your circumstances, to meet that inmost need?

Connecting Even in Crisis Is Good for Us

> "The capacity to preserve social connection . . . even in the face of extremity, seems to protect people to some degree against the later development of post-traumatic syndromes. For example, among survivors of a disaster at sea, the men who had managed to escape by cooperating with others showed relatively little evidence of post-traumatic stress afterward [whereas] highly symptomatic survivors were Rambos, men who had plunged into impulsive, isolated action and not affiliated with others."
>
> —*Psychiatrist Judith Herman*

"Lots of people saw television footage of the frantic sandbagging that went on a few years back when the Mississippi was trying to wash away a wide slice of the Midwest. What is a much harder story to show is the effect all that effort had on peoples lives. I live in one of those small towns that didn't fare so well, and in some ways I really believe that even with three feet of mud in my kitchen floor, I came out better for the experience.

"Our town had been going through some

trouble—nothing like the big cities—petty vandalism, budget problems that were dividing people up into camps, personal animosity that was beginning to surface—enough things to tarnish the small-town atmosphere that most of us had grown up in. When the waters started rising, all that was swept away. At one point, I was working ankle-deep in water and soaked to the bone right next to a guy I had a fight with three years before and hadn't spoken to since. We looked at each other and laughed. All that anger and built-up resentment just didn't mean a darn thing anymore."

We all know, because we have witnessed it over and over again, that crisis brings people together. Part of the reason is the obvious: In the face of such calamity, everything else pales. But perhaps a more important reason is that in a crisis we are suddenly and starkly reunited with the reality that we are all interdependent. We recognize the truth that the threads of that connection can never be broken.

Crisis is the wake-up call. So hopefully, in the ordinary days when we are tempted by the illusion that we can exist outside the community of others, we will remember.

Reap the Riches of Kindness

> "A man's true wealth is the good he does in the world."
>
> —*Mohammed*

"I was graphically reminded of the true value of life one day last year when I attended two funerals on the same day. The first was for the man who owned the company I worked for. He was a very wealthy man who had built his fortune with ruthless dedication. The funeral was a very sad affair, not because he had died, but because he had left so little of himself behind. There were no tears, no outpouring of grief, just a hollow ritual of death.

"The second funeral was for an old woman who had been a wonderful fixture in town for the past twenty years. She was kind of the town character, a woman without a family of her own but loved by everyone. She'd would go to the Little League baseball games and root for whichever side was losing; she'd dress up each Halloween and walk around town, waving at all the little kids. And she always had a smile and a nice word for every-one.

"Half the town turned out to say good-bye to her, and it turned into a movable party of remembrance, people remembering her antics, sharing our own favorite stories, and crying and laughing at the same time. She was a community treasure and will be sorely missed."

In a world where money seems to count for everything, it's so easy to lose track of what truly matters. Money can come and go, but nothing can touch the treasure we create in the loving of one another.

Our true wealth is counted in the goodwill we show and the lives we touch. So live richly and dispense your thoughtfulness freely.

Tend Your Spiritual Garden

> "To cultivate a beautiful garden you must uproot all weeds and all other unlovely things. Then you must plant and carefully cultivate in your mental garden seeds of kindness, goodness, love, purity, humility, reverence, and righteousness. As you persevere in this work your mind will gradually unfold into beauty and fragrance and your life will be blest."
>
> —*Grenville Kleiser*

"I guess everybody runs into people who don't like them, but for the longest time it seemed like most everyone had that reaction to me. It bothered me a lot but I always thought it was the other person's problem, until my best friend, Meagan, got really mad at me. For a few weeks, we didn't even talk, but finally I couldn't stand it so I asked her what was wrong. What Meagan told me was really hard to hear, because the more I thought about it, the more I realized she was right. I'm a pretty smart girl and I've always been proud of my brains, but now I know I need to learn how to be myself without making other people feel stupid. It makes me sad to think that there are people who I pushed away when they could have been my friends. But thanks to Meagan, at least now I know what I have been doing and I can work to change that."

We all grow up with our own garden of weeds. Shortness of temper, too quick retorts, impatience with others, a tendency to self-absorption, an inability to listen—we each have our own embarrassing list. But as we become more aware of what they are and how they affect others, we can prune the thorns, clear out the weeds, and plant seeds of consideration and compassion.

What weeds do you need to pull from your garden? Beating yourself up is not needed— all you need is a loving and gentle self-examination.

Place No Conditions on Compassion

> "Love thy neighbor, even when he plays the trombone."
>
> —*Jewish proverb*

"I was a pretty good athlete when I was in high school. I played varsity baseball and was one of the starters on the basketball team. My school was very into sports, so for a while there I was, a pretty important guy on campus. It was pretty heady stuff, and I think it actually might have done more damage than good if it weren't for this big klutz who befriended me.

"He was also on the basketball team, but only because he was really tall. He was your classic uncoordinated nerd, and half the team made fun of him; for some reason, he attached himself to me. Most of the time, it was really irritating, and I have to admit I wasn't always particularly nice to him. But then I'd feel guilty and try to lighten up a bit. I even found myself trying to include him more as part of the team during practices, and I think in some ways it helped all of us. He finally got to play during one of our last games, and when he scored the only two points he had ever scored, the whole team mobbed him on the sidelines.

"We never became really close friends, but when we graduated and everyone scattered to different schools, I realized that in a way I really missed him. His often irritating presence had made me grow up in ways that I don't think I would have even known about without him around."

True love is given with no strings attached—not just when you feel like it, not just when you get something back, not just when the other person appears worthy in your eyes. To be able to do this requires soul growth, and that is also its reward.

Give Fate a Helping Hand

> "It is the mark of a good action that it
> appears inevitable in retrospect."
> —*Anonymous*

We have a friend who was swimming with a group in Costa Rica, and just as the man next to her said, "I don't swim very well," she and he were swept far out to sea by a riptide. They were stranded for hours (he could float), as she tried to figure out how to get them both back in. Finally, she hatched a plan whereby he would hold onto one of her feet while she breaststroked back to shore. When we commented that it was incredible of her to stay and try to save him, risking her own life, she just shrugged and said, "Anyone would have done it."

We've noted before that when we were doing the *Random Acts of Kindness* series, we had trouble finding stories of the good deeds people had done themselves; everyone wanted to talk about the wonderful things others had done for them. We got very curious about that and tried to figure out why. When we asked people if they had ever done anything kind, they would invariably reply, "Well, yes, but it was no big deal because *any decent person would have done the same.*"

At its heart, the commission of a random act of kindness or any generous action doesn't seem special or extraordinary. It is purely and simply being willing to do what is obvious and necessary at any given moment—simply a matter of acting "decently," treating everyone as though they were a brother or sister who happens to be in need.

So do what seems obvious to you. It's okay if it is obvious; that is simply the clear bright path of kindness.

&mbrace the Feeling

> "When you carry out acts of kindness you get a wonderful feeling inside. It is as though something inside your body responds and says, Yes, this is how I ought to feel."
>
> —*Rabbi Harold Kushner*

"In my school we had some problems," writes a sixth grader. "A bunch of kids who thought they were really cool were being mean to people. One of the parents complained to the principal, and we all got a big lecture. So some kids started a club called 'It's Cool to Be Kind.' We'd do nice stuff like hold doors and help pick up books. I like the club and it has made my school a nicer place, but I do it because it feels good, not because I think it's cool."

Each of us, no matter our age, carries around inside a perfectly pure, self-regulating mechanism that guides us. It is our soul, our essence, telling us what is right and what is wrong. We simply need to clear away all the background noise so we can feel it.

When we reach out to others, our spirit

rings with the pure sweet resonance of a bell. It just feels "right," which is the acknowledgment that in that moment we are most truly and beautifully being ourselves.

So listen carefully today. Feel the chords of this beautiful inner song and you will make of your life a symphony for the world around you.

$\mathcal{T}$ake the Chance

> "What is the knocking? What is the knocking at the door in the night? It is somebody who wants to do us harm. No, no. It is three strange angels. Admit them, admit them."
>
> —Friedrich Holderlein

There were, amid all the atrocities of the Holocaust, those who dared to go against the terrible tide and help one another. This is just one of those stories.

In Poland, three Jews were hiding in a hut in the woods. Suddenly there was a knocking at door; fearing the Nazis, they were terrified to answer—they knew what the concentration camps held. But they also wondered if it were a fellow Jew needing help. So they decided to answer the door and discovered two injured Polish soldiers, their enemies, badly bleeding. Even though they had only a tiny bit of food, they shared what they had and nursed the soldiers back to health. When the soldiers were better, they used their knowledge and credentials to help their rescuers escape to safety.

We are constantly faced with choices in life. Most force us to choose between safety and risk. The risk in our lives is usually not as dramatic as it was for the people in this story. But it is risk nonetheless.

When we choose to open our hearts to another, we risk great pain and heartbreak. When we offer something of ourselves to another, we risk rejection. When we choose to stand up for what we believe, we risk ridicule or persecution. Sometimes, particularly in the moment when we must choose, the fear is so strong that it seems that we should simply retreat, choose to be safe. Yet in the instant we choose to be safe, we have already done ourselves the greatest harm, for we cut ourselves off from the potential of warmth and comfort from others.

We are brought into this world feeling helpless and alone. Our task is to consciously build the connections that will return us to the all-embracing heart of humanity. But we can find our way only if we are willing to take the chances we are offered.

Move to Your Soul

> "The principal thing in the world is to keep the soul aloft."
>
> —*Gustave Flaubert*

"Everybody calls it a 'midlife crisis,' but they are so wrong. We need to start calling it a 'midlife awakening' and then figure out how to teach our children better so that they never fall asleep in the first place.

"I am your classic example. I worked hard, stayed focused on what I thought was important, and did a darn good job of it at that. My midlife awakening came when I was forty years old and at the peak of my career. I just woke up one day and found I couldn't go on. I was miserable and depressed, and there just didn't seem to be any purpose to anything anymore. I spent three years searching, most of it in the wrong places and for the wrong things. I wanted something or someone to save me, to bring meaning back into my life. Finally, I gave up. Well, I guess I didn't really give up, I just wound down out of exhaustion, and there, in the silence of that exhaustion, I could finally feel my own heart welcoming me home."

We grow up being taught so many things, but somehow the most important lessons are all too often left out—like how to keep the soul afloat. We are all born with a holy purpose to fulfill, one that will nourish our spirit as we realize it.

How do we do this? Not just through work, or money, or success. Only through living in concert with our hearts, through giving freely in the spirit of loving-kindness can the soul take wing.

$\mathcal{A}$ Great Moral Force

"Twas a thief said the last kind word to Christ. Christ took the kindness and forgave the theft."

—Robert Browning

"My ex-husband called the other day. I hadn't seen him for years, and we ended up talking for nearly two hours. Our marriage had lasted only seven years and was a mess from the start. We argued and fought over everything, both of us were great at holding grudges and storing up resentment, and neither of us knew how to forgive. He called to apologize to me, and we ended up apologizing to each other for all the horrible, hurtful things we had put one another through.

"I used to believe my marriage was a mistake; now I see it as a gift. It was like we both needed to unleash all our selfish anger before we could find our true selves. My marriage made me so much bigger than I was; it taught me how to forgive."

We will all suffer at the hands or tongues of others in our lives. We will be emotionally robbed, battered, and victimized. We will not get what we need from a person we were counting on; we will get too much of what we don't need from those we are dependent on. But just like Christ with the thief who was hanging next to Him on the cross, we are all in this together. We have no idea where the kindness may come from. It could be from our equivalent of the thief, the person we've deemed as the one who has sinned against us the most.

And, unlike Christ, none of us is blameless; none of us will emerge with perfectly clean hands. We too will do our share of damage to those we supposedly love. We are, after all, human. And although it is our fate to be born with all the flaws and weaknesses of our kind, it is our destiny to learn from them that all can be washed away in the moment of forgiveness by the power of kindness.

The Grounding of Kindness

> "Love for what is near and small makes the sublime real and effective within our hearts."
>
> —José Ortega y Gasset

Many years ago, two friends began a journey to the sacred mountains, where they planned to meditate until they found God. On the way, they came across a small village that had been overtaken by a deadly disease. One of the men said, "I must stay here and help these people." His friend pleaded with him to go on with him, but he just said, "You go— I will catch up with you." The lone traveler continued on up into the mountains and spent many years in meditation and prayer, but his friend never came.

Thirty years went by, and word came through the mountains of the existence of a very holy man. The traveler determined to meet this man and seek out his wisdom for, despite all his efforts, he felt he never had the experience he longed for. After traveling many weeks, he came to a small village where the holy man was comforting the sick—and of course it was his long-lost friend. The traveler embraced his friend warmly and said, "Now I will stay with you; I have much catching up to do."

Many of us long for a transcendent mystical experience, an out-of-the ordinary event that will bring us rapture and ecstasy. Indeed, we can easily get caught up in wishing for a more soulful experience without having any idea of what that truly is.

In this parable, we are reminded that it is in the loving of that which is right in front of our noses that we come to know what the more lofty sentiments are. When we practice loving what is near, we get off the level of mushy sentimentality or abstract philosophy and sink into the soulful difficulty of the actuality. It is here, in the daily and often dull grind, in the offering of service to those around us, where we can truly find and express the deepest parts of our soul.

Know You Will Be Assisted

> "When a person's willing and eager, the gods join in."
>
> —*Aeschylus*

"It seems really dumb to say now, but I never realized I had so much control over my life. It always seemed to me that we were all just tiny cogs in the machinery of fate; some people were lucky, some weren't, and there was very little you could do about it. Since I was not one of the lucky ones, I found myself blaming others for my troubles. I blamed my parents, I blamed my parent's generation, I blamed my boss, the economy, and my ex-girlfriends. I blamed everyone and everything, and the more blame I dished out, the lower I sank.

"Finally, I screamed at God, 'Enough! I'm ready, I'm ready to change,' but even then I wanted change to happen because I had suffered enough, because I deserved it. Then one day, I realized I really *was* ready. I just wanted to let go and get on with my life. I threw away all the years of blaming, and almost immediately everything started to change. Wonderful, surprising people suddenly began to come into my life, and each day seemed full of opportunity."

We cannot force life into the mold and direction we demand. But when we open ourselves up and are willing to extend our hearts out into the world, the world will respond to us. It may not happen overnight, but slowly and surely it will begin to feel as though the universe was collaborating with us, rather than against us. And who knows? Maybe it is.

What Kindness Creates

> "Kindness in words creates confidence;
> kindness in thinking creates profound-
> ness; kindness in feeling creates love."
> —Lao Tzu

Lao Tzu's words remind us of the effects of kindness. When we speak kindly, we recall that this is who we truly are, a person of gentleness and warmth. In a world that is spinning so quickly, it is easy to lose track of the truth of our essence, to spin off into the distance until we no longer know who we are. Speaking words of kindness keeps us firmly in possession of our truth and gives us the confidence to go forward in the fullness of our authentic selves.

When we think kind thoughts, we open the channel that connects our mind to our heart. Gifted with such a marvelous tool as our intellect, we can easily become seduced by our own cleverness and become cut off from the depths of our heart. Thinking kind thoughts brings us back to our heart, where our deepest and most profound treasures are kept.

When we feel kindness, it connects us to our love for others. Our very nature as separate individuals makes it easy to forget how deeply and intricately we are all connected. Then we begin to feel isolated, as though we are completely alone in a world full of strangers. When we feel kindness, we are immediately connected to our love for those around us, because kindness is the medium of that love. We are thus reminded that we are not alone but, rather, no matter our circumstances, are nestled in the bosom of a loving family.

Observe your kind words, thoughts, and feelings as you go about your day and notice what effect they have on you.

Cultivate Joy

"Joy, divine spark of the Gods, / All men become brothers / where your gentle wings rest."

—*Schiller's "Ode to Joy"*

"The best teacher I ever had was a math teacher—and I hate math! He was such a happy, bubbly man it was infectious. Every morning, he would bound into the classroom like a golden retriever to greet us all with his quote of the day. Then somehow he managed to work the quote into whatever lesson we were doing that day. Once he had us all trying to figure out an algebraic formula to match the miracle of the loaves and fishes. We worked on it an entire class period, going around and around. When the class was over, he stood up with his usual beaming smile and said, 'You can't do it, because it was a miracle and miracles are not logical!' I never became terribly proficient in math, but I learned a lot about how much effect one soaring human spirit could have on those around him."

When we cultivate the joy we have inside

us, we carry it around with us like a bright lighthouse, spreading illumination on all we come in contact with. And while it is true that some people just naturally seem to have a sunnier disposition than others, we can learn to nourish and enhance that part of ourselves.

Sharing our joy and happiness with others brings us into the shelter of each other's hearts. So don't miss the golden opportunity to spread your joy around.

What Are You For?

"To work in the world lovingly means that we are defining what we will be for, rather than reacting to what we are against."
—*Christina Baldwin*

"I am a manager of a workgroup of about forty people. I always prided myself on my administrative skill. My style had always been very low-key, allowing people to establish their own approach, to work out their own problems, and intervening only when I felt it was necessary either to resolve disputes or redirect the approach. So when the company brought in an outside consultant to evaluate our group, I was confident that I would receive high marks.

"When I got the report, I was stunned to find out that over half my crew had major complaints about how I ran the operation. What was worse was that I was accused of doing the very things I was trying very hard not to do—micromanagement, displaying a general lack of confidence, setting people up to fail, and undermining group morale.

"At first I was hurt and angry, but the more

I read the anonymous comments, the more I realized where I had really screwed up. I had never clearly defined where I stood, never clearly articulated my vision of how we should be operating. Left in the dark, they not only came up with their own ideas—which I then would occasionally reject—but they also made up their own explanations for what I really wanted."

One of the central issues we struggle with throughout our lives is trying to reconcile the space between our individual selves and the deeper knowledge of our connection to all others. One of the most effective ways to bridge that gap is to turn ourselves inside out for the world to see. To fearlessly hold ourselves open for all to see is a great kindness to everyone around us. We show them the path to our hearts and give them the information they need to strengthen that connection.

When we hold back, we create fear and uncertainty. When we reveal what we stand for, we give others a starting place for relationship. What do you stand for in your life? Have you made that clear to those with whom you live and work?

What You Do Will Come Back to You

> "Every soul is the hostage of its own deeds."
>
> —*Koran*, 74:38

"One day at school, I found a 'Game Boy.' It was right there on the ground. I picked it up and looked around but couldn't see anyone who dropped it. I know I should have taken it to the principal's office, but I didn't. I took it home. I was going to play with it in my room, but my mind was bothering me. I was afraid something bad would happen to me because I took it. Instead of having fun, I was worried the whole time. I know I shouldn't have taken it home, so I promised God I would take it to the principal's office tomorrow. Nothing bad happened except I worried so much. I don't know if God heard me or not, but I learned my lesson."

Every religion has a belief that says, essentially: You will reap what you sow. Some have the idea of God as an ever-diligent judge watching over us to mete out punishment for our sins. Others believe in the law of karma, in which what you do—good or bad—will come back to you, if not in this lifetime then in another.

No matter how it is framed, it comes down to the same thing: If you do bad things, bad will come back to you; if you do good, you will receive good. All our actions and choices turn our lives down pathways where we will inevitably reap the seeds we have sown.

The truth is that it is an almost immediate effect. We don't need to wait for God's punishment or the next lifetime. When we make choices that lack compassion and integrity, we are already cutting ourselves off from the very things that we need to comfort and sustain us, whereas when we act with kindness and love, we bind ourselves more and more closely to the very things that can bring us delight and peace of mind.

So move kindly in the world, for your steps will take you exactly where you are headed.

Give Everything

"Everything that is not given is lost."
—*Indian proverb*

Read the above words again and really take them in: Everything that is not given is lost. It's a potent wake-up call.

Because we are mortal, every talent, skill, ability we possess, every thought and feeling we ever have, every beautiful sight we ever see, every material possession we own, will ultimately be lost. Unless we share it.

Unless we give what we have to others—to our spouse, to our child, to our friends and neighbors, to the strangers we encounter on our path—what we know and value will be irrevocably and utterly gone. But if we give freely of our minds and hearts and spirits, who we are and what matters to us will never die, but will live forever in the psyches of not only all those who know us, but everyone who encounters them, and then everyone who encounters those who knew them in an infinite regression of mysteriously unseen effect.

That's why the metaphor of a pebble in a pond is so potent. We toss the pebble of our soul into the pond of life and ripples are created. If we hoard ourselves, our gifts and talents, we will make a very little splash and the ripples soon end. But if we give fully, with abandon and abundance, the ripples go out infinitely, overlapping and intermingling with all other souls.

Viewed this way, what kind of ripple do you wish to be?

$\mathcal{T}$he Lens in the Beam

> "You are merely the lens in the beam. You can only receive, give and possess the light as the lens does. . . . You will know life and be acknowledged by it according to your degree of transparency, your capacity, that is, to vanish as an end, and remain purely as a means."
> —*Dag Hammarskjold*

There is a park is our neighborhood that was once the city's showpiece, but after years of budget cuts and changing neighborhoods, it had been allowed to deteriorate to the point that it not only was an eyesore but also had become dangerous. A man who grew up in this neighborhood and had become quite successful decided to do something about it. It took him five years, but he managed to bring the neighborhood together with the city planners and a number of community-based businesses to develop a plan to restore the park and ensure that it was maintained for years to come.

The real beauty of how he did it was that each step required a greater and greater involvement from the community itself, right down to a series of park renovation workdays where volunteers showed up to do a lot of the manual labor. When it was finished, there was a big celebration, and a huge crowd of proud neighbors turned out. The man who had set it all in motion was on vacation with his kids.

Like this man, we serve best when we hold clearly in mind the goal and purpose rather than our place in the process. Our ego might like to feel important, but it can often get in the way with its desire for self-aggrandizement. When we are able to be the lens, we help focus light where light is needed, and that is the greater reward.

ℒife's True Joy

"This is the true joy of life, the being used up for a purpose recognized by yourself as a mighty one; being a force of nature instead of a feverish, selfish little clot of ailments and grievances, complaining that the world will not devote itself to making you happy. I am of the opinion that my life belongs to the community, and as long as I live, it is my privilege to do for it what I can."

—*George Bernard Shaw*

"I grew up in a most dysfunctional family. Both my parents gave up long before I even got out of grammar school. I grew up surrounded by an impoverished alcoholic haze of bitterness and complaining. The message I was given was that the world is a nasty, dirty, unfair place that will take everything you have and give back nothing. If you wanted to survive, you had to beg, steal, and cheat to get whatever you could.

"How I managed to get out of that cesspool seems like a miracle to me sometimes. I know I was lucky to find people, good people, along the way who helped me to see the world differently, but in the end I think it was my parents who had the most influence in my life. All they ever thought of was their own selfish need, and all it ever got them was a life of complete misery. It took a lot of work, but I am on my own now and I have my own dream. It may not be a big dream, but I want to be a teacher so that maybe I can help some of the kids who have to go through what I went through."

We exist on two separate planes. The purely physical plane, where we appear for all purposes separate and apart, and the deeper spiritual plane, where we are beautifully and intricately bound up with the entirety of creation.

As this woman painfully discovered through her parent's lives, when we live solely for ourselves, we cut ourselves off from the spiritual plane and lose the only true source of meaning that exists. But when we live for and with others, we bring our physical manifestations closer into alignment with our deepest selves and live existences full of meaning, purpose, and joy.

$\mathcal{I}$n the End,
It's Very Simple

> "The beginning and end of Torah is performing acts of loving-kindness."
> —*The Talmud*

The *Torah* is the Jewish body of religious law, plus the first five books of the Bible. So the above quote is reminding us that all religious laws really come down to kindness, and that kindness is perhaps more important than any law. Here is a final story:

"I lived in a dorm my first year in college, and I had roommates who were like oil and water. Katherine had grown up in a very strict family. She didn't drink, smoke, or approve of dancing, and thought it was sinful to allow boys into our room. Melissa was kind of a wild child, a really sweet person with a great big heart. To her, life was like a grand experience to be savored. I was the bridge between them, impressed by Katherine's dedication and enchanted by Melissa's enthusiasm.

"By the end of the year, Katherine had enough, and Melissa and I ended up rooming together for the next few years. We hardly ever saw Katherine until one day during our senior year; I came home to find Katherine sitting on our couch, crying her eyes out. One of Melissa's great talents is that she always knows when people are upset, and she had stumbled onto a very distraught Katherine in the library and had immediately taken her under her wing. Katherine had fallen in love with a guy who very cruelly dumped her. "We ended up seeing a lot of Katherine that last semester. Melissa was there for her. In a strange way, it was a perfect closing of the circle that had started four years before."

None of us knows where and how kindness will come. The person whom we counted on may move to Tahiti; the person we hold in condemnation may end up being our salvation. The harder we try to hold on to rules and regulations, the more they seem to fail us.

In the end, all we can count on is ourselves—to come through as we can, when we can. If we make the commitment to kindness and have faith in the essential goodness of others, we *can* create a world of happiness and peace.

THE RANDOM ACTS OF KINDNESS FUND
Established 1994, Conari Press

Conari Press has made a commitment to donate 10% of the net proceeds from the sales of *The Pratice of Kindness* and the other books in the Kindness series to a Random Acts of Kindness fund. Part of that fund will go toward promoting National Random Acts of Kindness Week, including giving books away to children and adults who normally can't afford them. In compiling these books, we were struck by how often random acts of kindness involved homeless people; perhaps they are the group in our society that is most visibly in need.

Recognizing this, the greater portion of the fund will be given to VOLUNTEERS OF AMERICA, a national organization which helps relieve homelessness, and offers more than 400 programs in 339 communities nationwide. Here is a partial list of services they provide:

- AIDS support services
- Alcoholism prevention and treatment
- Apartments for the elderly and people with disabilities
- Congregate meals
- Counseling for individuals and families
- Day care for children
- Drug abuse prevention and treatment
- Employment assistance for ex-offenders, the homeless, people with disabilities and those in recovery
- Emergency shelters for the homeless
- Foster grandparents
- Group homes for people with developmental disabilities
- Home health care
- Literacy programs
- Long-term nursing care
- Meals delivered to the elderly and home-bound

If you would like more information about VOLUNTEERS OF AMERICA, please contact your local VOA organization, or call their national office at (800) 899-0089.

We thank you for your support of our books and this ideal, and want you to be aware that your purchase will continue the ripple of kindness. We can all make change happen. To request a free catalog of Conari Press books, please call us at (800) 685-9595 or write to: 2550 Ninth Street, Suite 101, Berkeley, CA 94710.